At a Glance

Paired Sources

Lee Brandon
Mt. San Antonio College

Houghton Mifflin Company   Boston   New York

To Sharon

Editor in Chief: Patricia A. Coryell
Senior Sponsoring Editor: Mary Jo Southern
Development Editor: Kellie Cardone
Editorial Assistant: Peter Mooney
Associate Project Editor: Christian Downey
Senior Manufacturing Coordinator: Marie Barnes
Marketing Manager: Annamarie Rice

Cover image: © 2002 Margaret Carsello/Images.com

Acknowledgments: Acknowledgments and copyrights continue on page 188, which constitutes an extension of the copyright page.

A. J. Anderson, "Sexual Harassment Is No Joke," from *Library Journal*, October 1, 1993, pp. 61–64. Copyright © 1993, used with permission of *Library Journal*, a publication of Cahners Business Information, a division of Reed Elsevier.

Maya Angelou, "Liked for Myself," from *I Know Why the Caged Bird Sings* by Maya Angelou, copyright © 1969 and renewed 1997 by Maya Angelou. Used by permission of Random House, Inc.

John Bowe, Marisa Bowe, and Sabin Streeter, from *Gig*. Copyright © 2000, 2001 by John Bowe, Marisa Bowe, and Sabin Streeter. Used by permission of Crown Publishers, a division of Random House, Inc.

Ellen Bravo and Ellen Cassedy, "Is It Sexual Harassment?" Reprinted by permission of Ellen Levine Literary Agency. From *The 9 to 5 Guide to Combating Sexual Harassment*, John Wiley & Sons. Revised and reissued by the National Association of Working Women, 1999. Copyright © 1992 by Ellen Bravo and Ellen Cassedy. Excerpt first published in *Redbook* Magazine, July 1992.

Copyright © 2003 by Houghton Mifflin Company. All rights reserved.

No part of this work may be reproduced or transmitted in any form or by any means, electronic or mechanical, including photocopying and recording, or by any information storage or retrieval system without the prior written permission of Houghton Mifflin Company unless such copying is expressly permitted by federal copyright law. Address inquiries to College Permissions, Houghton Mifflin Company, 222 Berkeley Street, Boston, MA 02116-3764.

Printed in the U.S.A.

Library of Congress Control Number: 2001133232

ISBN: 0-618-22190-5

123456789-FFG-06 05 04 03 02

Contents

Thematic Contents *viii*
Preface *xi*
Student Overview *xiii*

1 Writing: From Self to Sources 1

At a Glance: Writing Paragraphs and Essays 1
The Writing Process—Prewriting 1
The Writing Process—Writing, Revising, and Editing 2
The Paragraph and Its Parts 3
The Essay and Its Parts 4
Reading-Related Writing 6
Informal Documentation 8
Formal Documentation 8
Demonstration: Student Essay 9

   "My-graines" *Vincent Sheahan* 9

2 Narration: Moving Through Time 14

At a Glance: Using Narration in Writing 14

Paired Sources on Childhood Revisited 15

   "The Importance of Childhood Memories"
   Norman M. Lobsenz 15
   "What to a grown-up might seem a casual word or action often is, to a child, the kernel of a significant memory on which he or she will build."
   "Liked for Myself" *Maya Angelou* 19
   "For nearly a year, I sopped around the house, the Store, the school, and the church, like an old biscuit, dirty and inedible. Then I met, or rather got to know, the lady who threw me my first life line."

Topics for Using Narration in Writing 25

iv   Contents

3   Description: Moving Through Space   28

At a Glance: Using Description in Writing   28

Paired Sources on Restaurants—Food, Service, Ambiance   29

   "On the Road: A City of the Mind"   *Sue Hubbell*   29

   "They [tourists] file into the carpeted dining rooms away from the professional drivers' side, sit at the Formica tables set off by imitation cloth flowers in bud vases."

   "In the Land of 'Coke-Cola'"   *William Least Heat-Moon*   34

   "Inside, wherever an oddity or natural phenomenon could hang, one hung: stuffed rump of a deer, snowshoe, flintlock, hornet's nest. The place looked as if a Boy Scout troop had decorated it."

Topics for Using Description in Writing   39

4   Exemplification: Writing with Examples   41

At a Glance: Using Exemplification in Writing   41

Paired Sources on Loud Talking   41

   "Amid Backlash, Calls for Cell Phone Etiquette"   *Jennifer Oldham*   42

   "Secondhand cell phone conversations are fast replacing secondhand smoke as public enemy No. 1 in crowded venues nationwide."

   "The Talkies"   *James Lileks*   45

   "But people who talk in movies make me turn eight shades of mad. Plunk two talkers behind me and I start to pine for a decent billy club."

Topics for Using Exemplification in Writing   51

5   Analysis by Division: Examining the Parts   53

At a Glance: Using Analysis by Division in Writing   53

Paired Sources on What We Are—Heritage as Hyphenation   54

   "Growing Up Asian in America"   *Kesaya E. Noda*   54

   "I am my mother's daughter. And I am myself. I am a Japanese-American woman."

   "Intermarried . . . with Children"   *Jill Smolowe*   64

   "The land of immigrants may be giving way to a land of hyphenations, but the hyphen still divides even as it compounds."

Topics for Using Analysis by Division in Writing   70

Contents   v

6   Classification: Establishing Groups   73

At a Glance: Using Classification in Writing   73

Paired Sources on Ways of Controlling   74

"Why We Carp and Harp"   *Mary Ann Hogan*   74
"The hills are alive with the sound of nagging—the gnawing, crescendoing timbre of people getting in each other's face."

"How to Deal with a Difficult Boss"   *Donna Brown Hogarty*   79
"Most bosses were promoted to management because they excelled at earlier jobs—not because they have experience motivating others."

Topics for Using Classification in Writing   87

7   Process Analysis: Writing About Doing   90

At a Glance: Using Process Analysis in Writing   90

Paired Sources on McWorkers   91

"McDonald's—We Do It All for You"   *Barbara Garson*   91
"'And that's what it is, a machine. You don't have to know how to cook, you don't have to know how to think. There's a procedure for everything and you just follow the procedures.'"

"McDonald's Crew Member"   *Kysha Lewin*   95
"I know I can always get a job anywhere. The type of experience I got here, I can always get a job."

Topics for Using Process Analysis in Writing   100

8   Cause and Effect: Determining Reasons and Outcomes   102

At a Glance: Using Cause and Effect in Writing   102

Paired Sources on Love, Marriage, and Divorce   103

"Romantic Love, Courtship, and Marriage"   *Ian Robertson*   104
"A courtship system is essentially a marriage market. . . . Cupid's arrow, it turns out, does not strike at random."

"Why Marriages Fail"   *Anne Roiphe*   108
"Each of us falls in love with a mate who has qualities of our parents, who will help us rediscover both the psychological happiness and miseries of our past lives."

Topics for Using Cause and Effect in Writing   115

9 Comparison and Contrast: Showing Similarities and Differences 118

At a Glance: Using Comparison and Contrast in Writing 118

Paired Sources on Orderly and Disorderly People 120

"Neat People vs. Sloppy People" *Suzanne Britt* 120
"I've finally figured out the difference between neat people and sloppy people. The distinction is, as always, moral. Neat people are lazier and meaner than sloppy people."

"The Messy Are in Denial" *Joyce Gallagher* 124
"If they [messy people] are so contented, then why are so many of them latching onto and becoming entirely dependent on those of us who are organized?"

Topics for Using Comparison and Contrast in Writing 129

10 Definition: Clarifying Terms 131

At a Glance: Using Definition in Writing 131

Paired Sources on Sexual Harassment 132

"Is It Sexual Harassment?" *Ellen Bravo and Ellen Cassedy* 133
"Studies suggest that at least 50 percent of women experience sexual harassment at some point in their work or academic careers."

"Sexual Harassment Is No Joke" *A. J. Anderson* 140
"'There can be no doubt that Jason violated my personal space by telling a sexual joke. He showed great insensitivity. . . . I had no warning.'"

Topics for Using Definition in Writing 146

11 Argumentation: Writing to Persuade 148

At a Glance: Using Argumentation in Writing 148

Paired Sources on SUVs: 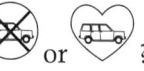 or ? 149

"SUVs: Killer Cars" *Ellen Goodman* 149
"The SUV backlash is growing so strong that today's status symbol may become the first socially unacceptable vehicle since cars lost their fins."

"Guzzling, Gorgeous & Grand: SUVs and Those Who Love Them" *Dave Shiflett* 152
"The fact is, we SUV drivers are peaceful, humble people of modest hopes and dreams, who happen to like driving around in large vehicles."

Topics for Using Argumentation in Writing   *158*

12   Mixed Patterns   *160*

At a Glance: Using Mixed Patterns in Writing   *160*

Paired Sources on Progress and Perspective   *160*

"The Seven Sustainable Wonders of the World"
 Alan Thein Durning   161
"To me, the real wonders are all the little things—little things that work, especially when they do it without hurting the earth."

"Listening to the Air"   *John (Fire) Lame Deer and Richard Erdoes   165*
"You have not only altered, declawed, and malformed your winged and four-legged cousins; you have done it to yourselves."

Reading-Related Topics for Writing About Progress and Perspective   *170*

Paired Sources on Freedom   *171*

"Sympathy"   *Paul Laurence Dunbar   172*
"When the wind stirs soft through the springing grass . . . I know why the caged bird sings!"

"The Story of an Hour"   *Kate Chopin   173*
"When she abandoned herself a little whispered word escaped her slightly parted lips. She said it over and over under her breath: 'Free, free, free!'"

Reading-Related Topics for Writing About Freedom   *177*

Paired Sources on the Impact of Possessions   *178*

"The Jacket"   *Gary Soto   178*
"My clothes have failed me. I remember the green coat that I wore in fifth and sixth grades when you either danced like a champ or pressed yourself against a greasy wall, bitter as a penny toward the happy couples."

"My Banana Car"   *Maria Varela   183*
"I got an image of the previous owner. He must have been a tall, heavy man who wore cheap cologne and liked horses."

Reading-Related Topics for Writing About the Impact of Possessions   *186*

Index   *189*

Thematic Contents

Childhood
What in your childhood shaped you, limited you, or strengthened you? What pivotal childhood experiences still live within you? What sweet or sour memories linger? How were the following authors affected in childhood? How does time change one's perception of events so that something that was once painful is now humorous, or something that seemed slight then is profoundly important now?

"The Importance of Childhood Memories"
  Norman M. Lobsenz   15

"Liked for Myself"   Maya Angelou   19

"Growing Up Asian in America"   Kesaya E. Noda   54

"The Jacket"   Gary Soto   178

"My Banana Car"   Maria Varela   183

Work
In what ways do work and the workplace define, limit, and change individuals? What can make life at work generally pleasant or unpleasant? Do the following sources remind you of any of your own work experiences?

"On the Road: A City of the Mind"   Sue Hubbell   29

"Why We Carp and Harp"   Mary Ann Hogan   74

"How to Deal with a Difficult Boss"
  Donna Brown Hogarty   79

"McDonald's—We Do It All for You"   Barbara Garson   91

"McDonald's Crew Member"   Kysha Lewin   95

"Is It Sexual Harassment?"   Ellen Bravo and
  Ellen Cassedy   133

"Sexual Harassment Is No Joke"   A. J. Anderson   140

Love
What do you really mean when you say "I love you" or "I don't love you anymore"? What are some sociological (group behavior) and

psychological (individual behavior) explanations for how love emerges and how it does or does not last?

"Intermarried ... with Children" *Jill Smolowe* 64

"Romantic Love, Courtship, and Marriage" *Ian Robertson* 104

"Why Marriages Fail" *Anne Roiphe* 108

"The Story of an Hour" *Kate Chopin* 173

The Confrontational Society
What behaviors or attitudes are viewed by society as obnoxious, and how are they related to freedom, respect for others, and responsibility? How can one complain in the most positive way? Or are the troubling situations mostly hopeless? How have you on specific occasions dealt with irritating situations?

"Amid Backlash, Calls for Cell Phone Etiquette" *Jennifer Oldham* 42

"The Talkies" *James Lileks* 45

"Why We Carp and Harp" *Mary Ann Hogan* 774

"How to Deal with a Difficult Boss" *Donna Brown Hogarty* 79

"Listening to the Air" *John (Fire) Lame Deer and Richard Erdoes* 165

"SUVs: Killer Cars" *Ellen Goodman* 149

"Guzzling, Gorgeous & Grand: SUVs and Those Who Love Them" *Dave Shiflett* 152

Gender
Judging from the following selections, can it be argued that a woman's life—social, work, and love—is, in some ways, more complicated and difficult than a man's? How are men represented in the following sources? To what extent are the representations fair?

"On the Road: A City of the Mind" *Sue Hubbell* 29

"Growing Up Asian in America" *Kesaya E. Noda* 54

"Why Marriages Fail" *Anne Roiphe* 108

"Is It Sexual Harassment?" *Ellen Bravo and Ellen Cassedy* 133

"Sexual Harassment Is No Joke" *A. J. Anderson* 140

"The Story of an Hour" *Kate Chopin* 173

Thematic Contents

Parents
What are some of the common pleasures and pains of raising children? How can parents (or guardians or surrogate parents) help prepare children to deal with problems that they will encounter in adulthood? How is parenting, good or bad, a significant concern in each of the following essays?

"The Importance of Childhood Memories" Norman M. Lobsenz 115

"Liked for Myself" Maya Angelou 19

"Growing Up Asian in America" Kesaya E. Noda 54

"Intermarried . . . with Children" Jill Smolowe 64

"Why We Harp and Carp" Mary Ann Hogan 74

"Why Marriages Fail" Anne Roiphe 108

Values
What values do you believe in, seek, promote, and cherish? How would you judge the values presented in the following selections?

"Liked for Myself" Maya Angelou 19

"Neat People vs. Sloppy People" Suzanne Britt 120

"The Messy Are in Denial" Joyce Gallagher 124

"The Seven Sustainable Wonders of the World" Alan Thein Durning 161

"Listening to the Air" John (Fire) Lame Deer and Richard Erdoes 165

"Sympathy" Paul Laurence Dunbar 172

Community
What constitutes a community? Is it only a neighborhood with geographical dimensions? Or can it be a group of people, even in different locations, who share the same experience, such as working, consuming, or struggling for survival.

"Liked for Myself" Maya Angelou 19

"On the Road: A City of the Mind" Sue Hubbell 29

"In the Land of 'Coke-Cola'" William Least Heat-Moon 34

"Growing Up Asian in America" Kesaya E. Noda 54

"McDonald's—We Do It All for You" Barbara Garson 91

"McDonald's Crew Member" Kysha Lewin 95

"The Jacket" Gary Soto 178

Preface

At a Glance: Paired Sources is the fourth-level book in the *At a Glance* series of concise English textbooks. Along with *At a Glance: Sentences, At a Glance: Paragraphs,* and *At a Glance: Essays,* it meets the current need for succinct, comprehensive, and up-to-date textbooks that students can afford. All four books provide basic instruction, exercises, and writing assignments at the designated level, as well as support material for instructors. *At a Glance: Sentences* and *At a Glance: Paragraphs* include a transition to the next level of writing, while *At a Glance: Paragraphs* and *At a Glance: Essays* end with a handbook to which students can refer for help with sentence-level issues or problems with mechanics. *At a Glance: Paired Sources* includes basic writing instruction and can be used by itself, with one of the other *At a Glance* books, or with another textbook. Two or more *At a Glance* books can be shrink-wrapped and delivered at a discount.

FEATURES
Concise Format
- Presents essential information in an abbreviated manner in order to produce a frugal textbook.

Comprehensive Instruction
- Contains twenty-six engaging sources with guide questions.
- Contains brief writing directions, including a student writing demonstration.
- Contains strategies for writing forms of discourse.
- Contains instructions for underlining and annotating reading material for better understanding.
- Contains basic directions for documented writing.
- Contains reading-related, career-related, and general writing topics.

Flexible and Engaging Material
- Has ten pairs of sources based on theme and pattern.
- Has three thematically united pairs with mixed patterns.

- Has individual sources, each of which can be discussed alone or in relation to its companion source.
- Has sources that give a range of perspectives with cultural diversity and gender balance, provide depth of thematic treatment, exemplify sound patterns, and demonstrate effective writing.
- Features celebrated authors such as Gary Soto, Maya Angelou, William Least Heat-Moon, Ellen Goodman, Paul Laurence Dunbar, Kate Chopin, and Suzanne Britt.

SUPPORT MATERIAL FOR INSTRUCTORS

- *Instructor's Guide.* Provides answers to exercises and quizzes. Quizzes may be photocopied and distributed to students.
- *Expressways 4.0* for PC, Macintosh, and Windows. Interactive software that guides students as they write and revise paragraphs and essays.

ACKNOWLEDGMENTS

I am profoundly indebted to the following instructors who have reviewed this textbook: Linda Clegg, Cerritos Community College; Lauri Humberson, St. Phillip's College; Carol Miter, Riverside Community College, Norco Campus; Richard Pepp, Massasoit Community College; Harvey Rubinstein, Hudson County Community College; Sylvia Stacey, Oakton Community College; Randa B. Wahbe, Pasadena City College; Suzanne Weisar, San Jacinto College, South Campus; Marian O'Shea Wernicke, Pensacola Junior College; and David Winner, Hudson County Community College.

Thanks also to members of the English department at Mt. San Antonio College, with special recognition to the Basic Courses Review Committee.

I deeply appreciate the work of freelance editors Ann Marie Radaskiewicz and Mary Dalton Hoffman, Nancy Benjamin of Books By Design, as well as my colleagues at Houghton Mifflin: Mary Jo Southern, Kellie Cardone, Annamarie Rice, Danielle Richardson, Peter Mooney, and Christian Downey.

I am especially grateful to my family of wife, children and their spouses, and grandchildren for their cheerful, inspiring support: Sharon, Kelly, Erin, Jeanne, Michael, Shane, Lauren, Jarrett, and Matthew.

Lee Brandon

Student Overview

At a Glance: Paired Sources contains thirteen pairs of sources that were selected to make you think and talk, show you useful ways to write effectively, and provide substance for writing assignments. Most pairs are grouped by both theme and form. The forms—for example, comparison and contrast, cause and effect, and argument—are commonly used in college writing tasks. The themes, which include sexual harassment, ways of controlling, and attitudes toward SUVs, are vital and relevant. The pair relationship varies. It may be pro and con. One source may be specific, the other general. One may define or interpret the other. One may echo the other, but with a different attitude. This arrangement naturally invites you to make connections, evaluate ideas, and call on your own experiences as you select or invent topics. The Thematic Contents suggests other relationships.

ORGANIZATION

Chapter 1
- Reading skills, including instructions on underlining and annotating
- The writing process, with student examples
- Instruction in summary writing and simple documentation
- A student demonstration showing you how to organize and write a reading-related essay

Chapters 2–11
- Ten pairs of sources dually grouped by theme and pattern of writing
- Consistent organization within each chapter

Example from Chapter 8:
> At a Glance: Using Cause and Effect in Writing
> (Study the concise listed discussion of each pattern to understand the pairs of sources. Later, use it as a checklist when writing your own composition.)

xiii

Paired Sources on Love, Marriage, and Divorce
(A brief introductory discussion will provide you with some perspective so you can make the connections between sources.)
"Romantic Love, Courtship, and Marriage"
"Why Marriages Fail"
(Pairs of reading selections are accompanied by guide questions and, usually, vocabulary study.)
Topics for Using Cause and Effect in Writing
(Suggested topics range from reading-related to career-related to general.)

Chapter 12

- Three pairs of sources with mixed patterns

LINKING READING AND WRITING

Here are some strategies to help you make the best use of this book and jump-start your reading and writing skills:

1. **Be active and systematic in learning.** Take advantage of your instructor's expertise by being an active participant in class—one who takes notes, asks questions, and contributes to discussion. Become dedicated to systematic learning: determine your needs, decide what to do, and do it. Make learning a part of your everyday thinking and behavior.
2. **Read widely.** Read to learn technique, to acquire ideas, to be stimulated to write. Especially read to satisfy your curiosity and to receive pleasure. If reading is a main component of your course, approach it as systematically as you do writing.
3. **Keep a journal.** Keeping a journal may not be required in your particular class, but whether required or not, it is a good idea to jot down your own ideas. Here are some topics for daily, or regular, journal writing:

   - Summarize, evaluate, or react to reading assignments.
   - Summarize, evaluate, or react to what you see on television and in movies, and to what you read in newspapers and in magazines.
   - Describe and narrate situations or events you experience.
   - Write about career-related matters you encounter in other courses or on the job.

Your journal entries may read like an intellectual diary, a record of what you are thinking about at certain times. Because your entries are not structured writing assignments, organization and editing are not important. Mainly, keeping a journal will help you to understand the material you read, to develop your language skills, to think more clearly, to become more confident, and to write more easily—so that writing itself becomes a comfortable everyday activity. Your entries may also provide subject material for longer, more carefully crafted pieces.

The most important thing is to get into the habit of writing something each day.

4. **Evaluate your writing skills.** Use the Self-Evaluation Chart inside the front cover of this book to list areas you need to work on. You can add to your lists throughout the entire term. Drawing on your instructor's comments, make notes on matters such as the organization, development, and content of your essays, spelling, vocabulary, and diction, and so on. Use the chart for self-motivated study assignments and as a checklist in all stages of writing. As you master each problem area, you can check it off or cross it out.

Here is a partially filled out Self-Evaluation Chart, with some guidelines for filling out your own.

Self-Evaluation Chart

Organization/ Development/ Content	Spelling/ Word Choice	Grammar/ Sentences	Punctuation/ Capitalization
Avoid top-heavy introductions Use specific examples Repeat key words such as *causes* and *effects*	all right separate sophomore avoid "into" as "into rap" "couldn't care less"	Vary sentence beginnings Watch for pronoun antecedent problems, such as "a person . . . they" RO/CS—*Then* isn't a conjunction	comma after long introductory modifier colon to introduce list cap beginning for words replacing names, such as, "I told Mother," but "I told my mother"

Organization/Development/Content. Note your instructor's suggestions for all aspects of planning your essays and supporting your ideas.

Spelling/Word Choice. List words marked as incorrectly spelled on your assignments. Master the words on your list and add new words as you accumulate assignments. List suggestions made by your instructor about word choice (such as avoiding slang, clichés, and vague terms). Also include new, useful words you encounter in this class and others; add the words here, with simple definitions. Use another page if you need more space.

Grammar/Sentences. List any grammar points you need to remember or any sentence problems, such as fragments, comma splices, and run-ons. If you tend to begin sentences in the same way or to use the same patterns, use your chart to remind yourself to vary your sentence beginnings and patterns.

Punctuation/Capitalization. List any problems you encounter with punctuation or capitalization.

5. **Be positive.** Don't compare yourself with others. Compare yourself with yourself, and as you make progress, consider yourself what you are—a student on the path toward effective writing, a student on the path of success.

1

Writing: From Self to Sources

At a Glance: Writing Paragraphs and Essays

THE WRITING PROCESS—PREWRITING

1. The writing process consists of strategies that can help you produce a polished essay. **Prewriting** includes exploring experimenting, gathering information, writing the controlling idea, and organizing and developing support. **Writing** includes drafting, revising, and editing.
2. Prewriting covers one or more of the following strategies:

    Freewriting: writing without stopping so that you can explore, experiment, and invent

    Brainstorming or listing: responding to *Who? What? Where? When? Why?* and *How?* questions or making lists on likely divisions of your subject

    Clustering: showing related ideas by "double-bubbling" a subject and then connecting single bubbles of related ideas on spokes radiating out and branching from the hub

    Gathering information: can take the form of underlining, annotating, and note taking

    Composing the topic sentence or thesis: writing a sentence that has two parts—the subject (what you are writing about) and the treatment (what you will do with the subject)

    Outlining: dividing the controlling idea into sections of support material, dividing those sections further, and establishing a workable sequence

The Writing Process—Writing, Revising, and Editing

1. Writing
   Write your first draft, paying close attention to your outline or list or cluster. Do not concern yourself with perfect spelling, grammar, or punctuation.
2. Revising

   Coherence
   - Are the ideas clearly related, each one to the others, and to the central idea?
   - Is there a clear pattern of organization (time, space, or emphasis)?
   - Is the pattern supported by words that suggest the basis of that organization (time: *now, then, later*; space: *above, below, up, down*; emphasis: *first, second, last*)?
   - Is coherence enhanced by the use of transitional terms, pronouns, repetition, and a consistent point of view?

   Language
   - Is the general style of language usage appropriate (properly standard and formal or informal) for the purpose of the piece and the intended audience?
   - Is the tone (language use showing attitude toward material and audience) appropriate?
   - Is the word choice (diction) effective? Are the words precise in conveying meaning? Are they fresh and original?

   Unity
   - Is the thesis and every topic sentence clear and well stated? Do they indicate both subject and treatment?
   - Are all points of support clearly related to and subordinate to the topic sentence of each paragraph and to the thesis of the essay?

   Emphasis
   - Are ideas properly placed (especially near the beginning and end) for emphasis?
   - Are important words and phrases repeated for emphasis?

Support
- Is there adequate material—such as examples, details, quotations, and explanations—to support each topic sentence and the thesis?
- Are the points of support placed in the best possible order?

Sentence Structure
- Are the sentences varied in length and beginnings?
- Are the sentences varied in pattern (simple, compound, complex, and compound-complex)?
- Are all problems with sentence structure (fragments, comma splices, run-ons) corrected?

3. Editing
- Are all problems in such areas as capitalization, omissions, punctuation, and spelling corrected?

THE PARAGRAPH AND ITS PARTS

1. The **developmental paragraph** is a group of sentences, each with the function of stating or supporting a controlling idea called the **topic sentence**.
2. The developmental paragraph contains three parts: the subject, the topic sentence, and the support.
3. The two main patterns of the developmental paragraph are these:

Pattern A

Topic Sentence

Support

Support

Support

Development

Pattern B

Topic Sentence

Support

Support

Support

Concluding Sentence

Development

4. The topic sentence includes what you are writing about—the **subject**—and what you intend to do with that subject—the **treatment**.

<u>Being a good parent</u> is more than providing financial support.
      subject   treatment

5. The **outline** is a pattern for showing the relationship of ideas. It can be used to reveal the structure and content of something you read or to plan the structure and content of something you intend to write. The following topic outline shows how the parts are arranged on the page as well as how the ideas in it relate to one another.

Main Idea (will usually be the topic sentence for the paragraph or the thesis for the essay)
  I. Major support
    A. Minor support
      1. Details (specific information of various kinds)
      2. Details
    B. Minor support
      1. Details
      2. Details
 II. Major support
    A. Minor support
    B. Minor support
      1. Details
      2. Details
      3. Details
Concluding sentence (optional)

THE ESSAY AND ITS PARTS

1. An **essay** is a group of paragraphs, each of which supports a controlling statement called a **thesis**.
2. An effective thesis has both a subject and a treatment.

    The subject is what you intend to write about.

    The treatment is what you intend to do with your subject.

    EXAMPLE: <u>Bidwell Elementary School</u> <u>is too crowded.</u>
                            subject   statement

3. An effective thesis presents a treatment that can be developed with supporting information.

4. An ineffective thesis is vague, too broad, or too narrow.
5. Each paragraph in an essay is almost always one of three types: introductory, support, or concluding.
6. A good introductory paragraph attracts the reader's interest, states or points toward the thesis, and moves the reader smoothly into the support, or body, paragraphs.
7. Introductory methods include a direct statement of the thesis, background, definition of term(s), quotation(s), a shocking statement, question(s), and a combination of two or more methods in this list.
8. Supporting information is often presented in patterns, such as narration, cause and effect, analysis by division, and process analysis.
9. Your concluding paragraph should give the reader the feeling that you have said all you want to say about your subject.
10. Some effective methods of concluding are a restatement of the thesis in slightly different words, perhaps pointing out its significance or making applications of it; a review of the main points; an anecdote related to the thesis; and a quotation.

The essay can often be considered an amplification of a developmental paragraph.

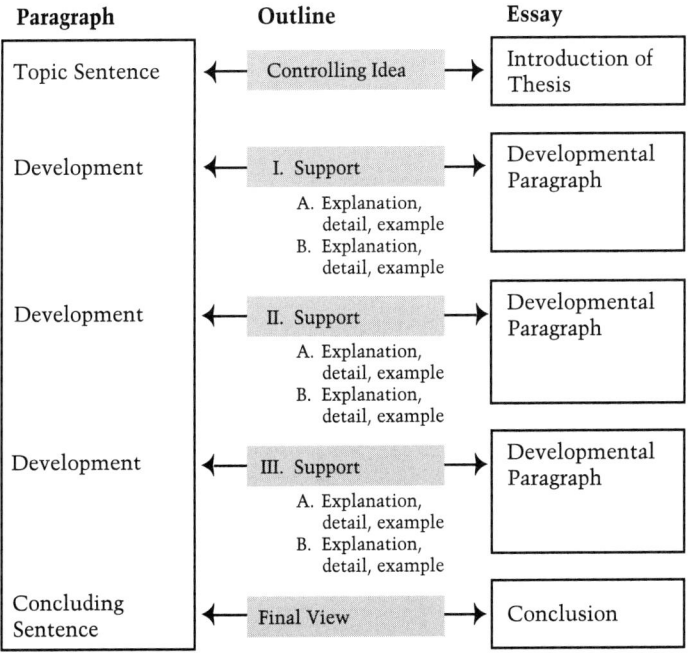

READING-RELATED WRITING

Because most college writing assignments are connected with reading, it is worthwhile to consider how to focus thoughtful attention on the written word. Of course, if you know about writing assignments or tests beforehand, your reading can be more concentrated. You should always begin a reading assignment by asking yourself why you are reading that particular material and how it relates to your course work and interests. For example, most selections in this book are presented as ideas to stimulate thought and invite reflective comparisons, to provide material for analysis and evaluation, and to show how a pattern or process of writing can be done effectively. The discussion and critical thinking questions and activities that follow the selections arise from these purposes. Other questions raised by your instructor or on your own can also direct you in purposeful reading. Consider such questions and activities at the outset. Then, as you read, use strategies that are appropriate for the kind of assignment you are working on.

1. *Underlining* helps you to read with discrimination.
   - Underline the main ideas in paragraphs.
   - Underline the support for those ideas.
   - Underline answers to questions that you bring to the reading assignment.
   - Underline only the key words.

2. *Annotating* enables you to actively engage the reading material.
   - Number parts if appropriate.
   - Make comments according to your interests and needs.

In Bed

Joan Didion

<ul style="list-style:none">
<li>It was a long time before I began thinking mechanistically enough to <u>accept migraine for what it was:</u></li>
<li>Chronic — something with which I would be living, <u>the way some people live with diabetes.</u> <u>Migraine</u> is something <u>more than</u> the fancy of <u>a neurotic imagination.</u></li>
<li>Hereditary — It is an essentially <u>hereditary complex of symptoms,</u> the <u>most frequently noted</u> but by no means the</li>
<li>Main symptom — most unpleasant of which is a <u>vascular headache</u> of <u>blinding severity,</u> <u>suffered by</u> a surprising number of</li>
</ul>

women, a fair number of men (Thomas Jefferson had migraine, and so did Ulysses S. Grant, the day he accepted Lee's surrender), and by some unfortunate children as young as two years old. . . . Almost anything can trigger a specific attack of migraine: stress, allergy, fatigue, an abrupt change in barometric pressure, a contretemps over a parking ticket. A flashing light. A fire drill. One inherits, of course, only the predisposition. In other words I spent yesterday in bed with a headache not merely because of my bad attitudes, unpleasant tempers and wrongthink, but because both my grandmothers had migraine, my father has migraine and my mother has migraine.

Trigger varies— for me too—

Only my uncle?

3. *Outlining* the passages you read sheds light on the relationship of ideas, including the major divisions of the passage and their relative importance.
4. *Summarizing* helps you concentrate on main ideas. A summary
   - cites the author and title of the text.
   - is usually shorter than the original by about two-thirds, although the exact reduction will vary depending on the content of the original.
   - concentrates on the main ideas and includes details only infrequently.
   - changes the original wording without changing the idea.
   - does not evaluate the content or give an opinion in any way (even if you see an error in logic or fact).
   - does not add ideas (even if you have an abundance of related information).
   - does not include any personal comments by the author of the summary (therefore, no use of *I* referring to self).
   - seldom uses quotations (but if you do, only with quotation marks).
   - uses some author tags ("says York," "according to York," or "the author explains") to remind the reader(s) that you are summarizing the material of another writer.
5. Two other types of reading-related writing are
   - the *reaction*—how the reading relates to you, your experiences, and your attitudes; also, often your critique of the worth and logic of the piece.

- the *two-part response*—separates a summary from a reaction.
6. Most ideas in reading-related papers are developed in one or more of these three ways:
   - explanation
   - direct references
   - quotations
7. *Documenting* is giving credit to borrowed ideas and words.

Informal Documentation

If you are writing in response to material in your textbook, especially if it is a single source, your instructor may not require you to indicate by page number where you found each borrowed idea. However, you will be expected to make clear (by use of quotation marks and by the name of an author, the title of the selection, or both name and title) that you have borrowed ideas. Simply writing something such as "I agree with Suzanne Britt when she says in 'Neat People vs. Sloppy People' that disorganized people have good intentions" would suffice. This style of acknowledgment is commonly called informal documentation. It is often used in college writing when both writer and readers have familiarity with and shared access to the sources. Informal documentation also is commonplace in newspaper and periodical articles.

Formal Documentation

Documenting sources for papers based on written material is usually quite simple. One popular documentation method is MLA (Modern Language Association) style. Here are its most common principles that can be used for textbook or other restricted sources, with some examples.

- If you use material from a source you have read, identify that source so the reader will recognize it or be able to find it.
- Document any original idea borrowed, whether it is quoted, paraphrased (written in your words but not shorter), or summarized (written in your words and shorter). Basic situations include the following:

   Normally, you need give only the author's name and a page number: (Rivera 45).

If you state the author's name in introducing the quotation or idea, then usually give only the page number: (45).

If the author has written more than one piece in the book, then a title or shortened form of the title is also required: (Rivera, *The Land* 45).

Here is an example of documenting a quotation by an author represented only once in a textbook.

- Using the author's name to introduce:

    Suzanne Britt says that "neat people are bums and clods at heart" (255).

Following is an example of documenting an idea borrowed from an author but not quoted.

- Using the author's name to introduce:

    Suzanne Britt believes that neat people are weak in character (255).

- Not using the author's name to introduce:

    Music often helps Alzheimer's patients think more clearly (Weiss 112).

DEMONSTRATION: STUDENT ESSAY

My-graines

Vincent Sheahan

The assignment was to read an essay related to health and write a documented essay of extended definition about a health condition as it related to the student's experience. (Your instructor may not ask you to formally document an essay based on a single source found in your textbook; instead, clear references and accurate use of quotations marks would suffice.)

```
    The aura set in like a suffocating
stillness before a tropical storm. "This is
going to be a bad one," I told myself as I
shut off the lights, took my medication, lay
```

down, and prepared for the inevitable--the relentless throbbing in my temple. About three hours of incapacitating agony later, I recovered, feeling strangely drained, and skimmed through my reading assignment for my college English class. What a coincidence! It included "In Bed," an essay about migraines by Joan Didion. Because I had only recently been diagnosed with migraines (although I had long suffered), I naturally had enormous curiosity about the subject, and now homework coincided

Thesis with my private need for information. <u>By closely comparing my family history, my triggers for attacks, and my personality with Joan Didion's, perhaps I could find some informed answers to my questions and be able to define "migraines" more precisely.</u>

Topic sentence <u>A year ago when I decided to seek medical help, the matter of family history was of immediate concern.</u> At my first appointment, my neurologist informed me that, although no one knows why, migraines tend to run in families. I said the only person in my family who has migraines is my Uncle Joe, my father's brother. For Didion, the family connection is more apparent and pervasive: Both of her grandmothers, her father, and her mother all suffer from migraine headaches.

But she does go on to explain, "One inherits, of course, only the predisposition" (59). Therefore, it is possible that everyone on my father's side has carried the gene for migraines but only Uncle Joe has developed the headaches.

Topic sentence After the doctor asked his questions, I had one of my own: What actually causes migraine headaches? I was fearful that my job as an emergency medical technician (E.M.T.), with its debilitating stress and irregular hours, was the main reason. He explained that the exact causes are not completely understood and that my fatigue and irregular sleep patterns are not the causes of my migraines, because there are plenty of E.M.T.'s who have the same sleep patterns as I do, yet do not have migraines. Nevertheless, the fatigue and irregular sleep may trigger migraine headaches. For Didion, the triggers are varied. She says, "Almost anything can trigger a specific attack of migraine: stress, allergy, fatigue, an abrupt change in barometric pressure, a contretemps over a parking ticket. A flashing light. A fire drill" (60). Yet she explains that her headaches are not triggered at times when she needs to be alert and thinking clearly, such as an emergency situation, but instead, they are triggered when she is feeling overwhelmed or extremely stressed (60).

Topic sentence — In addition to the exposure to these triggers, a migraine sufferer like me usually has what is called a "migraine personality." Didion offers a good definition of that term, saying that she is typical, a perfectionist who is "ambitious, inward, intolerant of error, rather rigidly organized" (60). But she points out that not all perfectionists have migraines and not all people with migraines are perfectionists. She says that she is a perfectionist about writing, not housekeeping (60). And as for me, I try-- probably harder than most--to be organized when it comes to my education, work, and personal life.

Like Joan Didion, I am intensely interested in migraines, and I am learning about them. We migraine sufferers have much in common, though each of us has his or her own family history of migraines, triggers, and migraine personality. Knowing that others go though what I do and having more information about my condition make it easier for me to deal with the pain of my migraines. I will continue to do the same thing Joan

Demonstration: Student Essay 13

```
Didion does when she has an aura: I won't try
to fight it. I will lie down and endure. When
it's finally over, I will count my blessings.
```

> Vincent Sheahan's instructor asked him to include a citation of his source in MLA form. It is annotated to indicate parts.

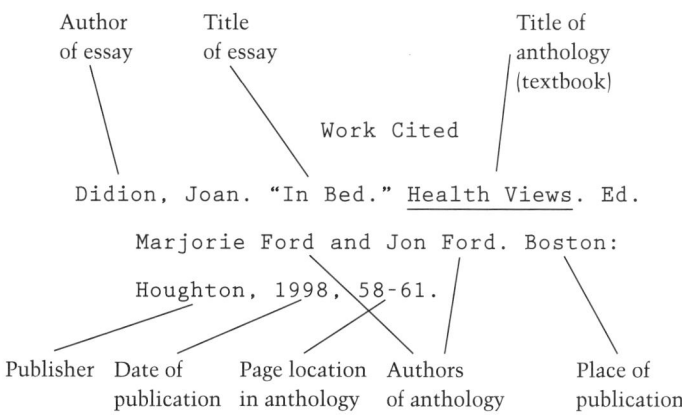

> Here is the same MLA form applied to a source from this textbook.
>
> Gallagher, Joyce. "The Messy Are in Denial." *At a Glance: Paired Sources.* Ed. Lee Brandon. Boston: Houghton, 2002. 124–127.

2

Narration: Moving Through Time

At a Glance: Using Narration in Writing

1. Include these points so you will be sure you have a complete narrative:
   - situation (what's going on)
   - conflict (problem to be dealt with)
   - struggle (dealing with problem)
   - outcome (result of dealing with problem)
   - meaning (significance or point)
2. Use these techniques or devices as appropriate:
   - images that appeal to the senses (sight, smell, taste, hearing, touch) and other details to advance action
   - dialogue (conversation)
   - transitional devices (such as *next, soon, after, later, then, finally, when, following*) to indicate chronological order
3. Give details concerning action.
4. Be consistent with point of view (*I* for first person or *he, she,* or *it* for third person) and verb tense (*is* for present and *was* for past).
5. Keep in mind that most narratives written as college assignments will have an expository purpose; that is, they explain a specific idea.
6. Consider working with a limited time frame for short writing assignments. That is, the scope would usually be no more than one

incident of brief duration for one paragraph. For example, writing about an entire graduation ceremony might be too complicated, but concentrating on the moment when you walked forward to receive the diploma or the moment when the relatives and friends come down on the field could work very well.

> **PAIRED SOURCES ON CHILDHOOD REVISITED**
>
> As we grow older, we often reflect on our childhood and find a seedbed of experiences that have enhanced or haunted our lives. Those recollections will always be with us, and as parents and grandparents we may share them with others as colorful stories. Of course, they are more than little disjointed tales; they indicate what made us who we are. In this pair of sources, Norman M. Lobsenz and Maya Angelou recount indelible events in their lives, and in doing so reveal themselves.

The Importance of Childhood Memories
Norman M. Lobsenz

A freelance writer, Norman M. Lobsenz uses several shorter narratives to illustrate his point that childhood experiences influence adult values, stability, and character. This essay first appeared in Reader's Digest.

1 Some years ago, when my young wife became desperately ill, I wondered how I would be able to cope with the physical and emotional burdens of caring for her. One night, when I was drained of strength and endurance, a long-forgotten incident came to mind.

2 I was about ten years old at the time and my mother was seriously ill. I had gotten up in the middle of the night to get a drink of water. As I passed my parents' bedroom, I saw the light on. I looked inside. My father was sitting in a chair in his bathrobe next to Mother's bed, doing nothing. She was asleep. I rushed into the room.

3 "What's wrong?" I cried. "Why aren't you asleep?"

4 Dad soothed me. "Nothing's wrong. I'm just watching over her."

5 I can't say exactly how, but the memory of that long-ago incident gave me the strength to take up my own burden again.

The remembered light and warmth from my parents' room were curiously powerful and my father's words haunted me: "I'm just watching over her." The role I now assumed seemed somehow more bearable, as if a resource had been called from the past or from within.

6 In moments of psychological jeopardy, such childhood memories often turn out to be the ultimate resources of personality, dark prisms which focus our basic feeling about life. As Sir James Barrie once wrote, "God gives us memory so that we may have roses in December."

7 No parent can ever really know which memory, planted in childhood, will grow to be a rose. Often our most vivid and enduring remembrances are of apparently simple, even trivial things. I did not discover this myself until one bright, leaf-budding spring day when my son Jim and I were putting a fresh coat of paint on the porch railing. We were talking about plans to celebrate his approaching fifteenth birthday, and I found myself thinking how quickly his childhood had passed.

> **No parent can ever really know which memory, planted in childhood, will grow to be a rose.**

8 "What do you remember best?" I asked him.

9 He answered without a moment's hesitation. "The night we were driving somewhere, just you and me, on a dark road, and you stopped the car and helped me catch fireflies."

10 Fireflies? I could have thought of a dozen incidents, both pleasant and unpleasant, that might have remained vivid in his mind. But fireflies? I searched my memory—and eventually it came back to me.

11 I'd been driving cross-country, traveling late to meet a rather tight schedule. I had stopped to clean the windshield, when all at once a cloud of fireflies surrounded us. Jim, who was five years old then, was tremendously excited. He wanted to catch one. I was tired and tense, and anxious to get on to our destination. I was about to tell him that we didn't have time to waste when something changed my mind. In the trunk of the car I found an empty glass jar. Into it we scooped dozens of the insects. And while Jim watched them glow, I told him of the mysterious cold light they carried in their bodies. Finally, we uncapped the jar and let the fireflies blink away into the night.

12 "Why do you remember that?" I asked. "It doesn't seem terribly important."
13 "I don't know," he said. "I didn't even know I did remember it until just now." Then a few moments later: "Maybe I do know why. Maybe it was because I didn't think you were going to stop and catch any with me—and you did."
14 Since that day I have asked many friends to reach back into their childhoods and tell me what they recall with greatest clarity. Almost always they mention similar moments—experiences or incidents not of any great importance. Not crises or trauma or triumphs, but things which although small in themselves carry sharp sensations of warmth and joy, or sometimes pain.
15 One friend I spoke with was the son of an executive who was often away from home. "Do you know what I remember best?" he said to me. "It was the day of the annual school picnic when my usually very dignified father appeared in his shirtsleeves, sat on the grass with me, ate a box lunch, and then made the longest hit in our softball game. I found out later that he postponed a business trip to Europe to be there."
16 My friend is a man who experiences the world as a busy, serious place but who basically feels all right about it and about himself. His favorite childhood memory is both clue to and cause of his fundamental soundness.
17 Clearly, the power parents have to shape the memories of their children involves an awesome responsibility. In this respect nothing is trivial. What to a grown-up might seem a casual word or action often is, to a child, the kernel of a significant memory on which he or she will build. As grownups, we draw on these memories as sources of strengths or weaknesses. Author Willa Cather saw this clearly. "There are those early memories," she wrote. "One cannot get another set; one has only those."
18 Not long ago, I talked to a woman who has married a young and struggling sculptor. She cheerfully accepted their temporary poverty. "I grew up during the depression," she said. "My dad scrambled from one job to another. But I remembered that each time a job ended, my mother would scrape together enough money to make us an especially good dinner. She used to call them our 'trouble meals.' I know now that they were her way of showing Dad she believed in him, in his ability to fight

back. I learned that loving someone was far more important than having something."

19 If childhood memories are so important, what can parents do to help supply their children with a healthy set?

20 • For one thing, parents should be aware of the importance of the memory-building process. In our adult preoccupation, we tend to think that the "important" experiences our children will have are still in their future. We forget that, to them, childhood is reality rather than merely a preparation for reality. We forget that childhood memories form the adult personality. "What we describe as 'character,' " wrote Sigmund Freud, "is based on the memory traces of our earliest youth."

21 • Parents can try to find the extra energy, time, or enthusiasm to carry out the small and "insignificant" plan that is so important to a child. The simple act of baking that special batch of cookies or helping to build that model car, even though you are tired or harried, may make an important memory for your youngster.

22 Conversely, parents can try to guard against the casual disillusionments and needless disappointments which they often unthinkingly inflict on children. I would venture that almost everyone has a memory of an outing canceled or a promise broken without a reason or an explanation. "My father always used to say, 'We'll see,' " one man told me. "I soon learned that what that meant was 'no,' but without any definite reason."

23 • Parents can keep up family traditions and rituals. Simple observations that may not seem terribly important to a grown-up can be enormously meaningful to a child. A ritual walk in the woods on the first day of spring, a family dinner on someone's birthday, these are often significant to a youngster long past the time we might think he or she stopped caring about them.

24 • Parents can think back to their own childhoods and call up their own memories. By remembering the incidents that made important impressions on them, parents can find guideposts to ways in which they can shape the future memories of their own youngsters.

25 • Finally, parents can by their own actions and words communicate emotions as well as experiences to their children. We can give them a memory of courage rather than fear; of

strength rather than weakness; of an appetite for adventure rather than a shrinking from new people and places; of warmth and affection rather than rigidity and coldness. In just such memories are rooted the attitudes and feelings that characterize a person's entire approach to life.

> **EXERCISE 1   Discussion and Critical Thinking**

1. Narratives, especially in college writing, are usually intended to illustrate some idea: an influence, a value, or a common behavior. To what purpose does Lobsenz use his short narratives in this essay?

2. The author twice uses an analogy to a rose to show the benefits of childhood memories. In terms of what the author is trying to say, why does he emphasize the flowers of the rose plant rather than the thorns?

3. In the first narrative used by Lobsenz (paragraphs 1–6), what are the basic parts: the situation, conflict, struggle, outcome, and meaning?

Liked for Myself

Maya Angelou

As a child, Maya Angelou (Marguerite), author of the autobiographical book I Know Why the Caged Bird Sings, *was raped by a friend of her mother. In this excerpt she has only recently come to live in her grandmother's home in rural Stamps, Arkansas. There, psychologically wounded by her experience, she does not speak. She is desperate for self-confidence. She needs to be liked for the person she is.*

1   For nearly a year, I sopped around the house, the Store, the school, and the church, like an old biscuit, dirty and inedible. Then I met, or rather got to know, the lady who threw me my first life line.

2   Mrs. Bertha Flowers was the aristocrat of Black Stamps. She had the grace of control to appear warm in the coldest weather, and on the Arkansas summer days it seemed she had a private breeze which swirled around, cooling her. She was thin without the taut look of wiry people, and her printed voile dresses and flowered hats were as right for her as denim overalls for a farmer. She was our side's answer to the richest white woman in town.

3   Her skin was a rich black that would have peeled like a plum if snagged, but then no one would have thought of getting close enough to Mrs. Flowers to ruffle her dress, let alone snag her skin. She didn't encourage familiarity. She wore gloves too.

4   I don't think I ever saw Mrs. Flowers laugh, but she smiled often. A slow widening of her thin black lips to show even, small white teeth, then the slow effortless closing. When she chose to smile on me, I always wanted to thank her. The action was so graceful and inclusively benign.

5   She was one of the few gentlewomen I have ever known, and has remained throughout my life the measure of what a human being can be. . . .

6   One summer afternoon, sweet-milk fresh in my memory, she stopped at the Store to buy provisions. Another Negro woman of her health and age would have been expected to carry the paper sacks home in one hand, but Momma said, "Sister Flowers, I'll send Bailey up to your house with these things."

7   She smiled that slow dragging smile, "Thank you, Mrs. Henderson. I'd prefer Marguerite, though." My name was beautiful when she said it. "I've been meaning to talk to her, anyway." They gave each other age-group looks. . . .

8   There was a little path beside the rocky road, and Mrs. Flowers walked in front swinging her arms and picking her way over the stones.

9   She said, without turning her head, to me, "I hear you're doing very good school work, Marguerite, but that it's all written. The teachers report that they have trouble getting you to talk in class." We passed the triangular farm on our left and the path widened to allow us to walk together. I hung back in the separate unasked and unanswerable questions.

10 "Come and walk along with me, Marguerite." I couldn't have refused even if I wanted to. She pronounced my name so nicely. Or more correctly, she spoke each word with such clarity that I was certain a foreigner who didn't understand English could have understood her.

11 "Now no one is going to make you talk—possibly no one can. But bear in mind, language is man's way of communicating with his fellow man and it is language alone which separates him from the lower animals." That was a totally new idea to me, and I would need time to think about it.

12 "Your grandmother says you read a lot. Every chance you get. That's good, but not good enough. Words mean more than what is set down on paper. It takes the human voice to infuse them with the shades of deeper meaning."

13 I memorized the part about the human voice infusing words. It seemed so valid and poetic.

14 She said she was going to give me some books and that I not only must read them, I must read them aloud. She suggested that I try to make a sentence sound in as many different ways as possible.

15 "I'll accept no excuse if you return a book to me that has been badly handled." My imagination boggled at the punishment I would deserve if in fact I did abuse a book of Mrs. Flowers'. Death would be too kind and brief.

16 The odors in the house surprised me. Somehow I had never connected Mrs. Flowers with food or eating or any other common experience of common people. There must have been an outhouse, too, but my mind never recorded it.

17 The sweet scent of vanilla had met us as she opened the door.

18 "I made tea cookies this morning. You see, I had planned to invite you for cookies and lemonade so we could have this little chat. The lemonade is in the icebox."

19 It followed that Mrs. Flowers would have ice on an ordinary day, when most families in our town bought ice late on Saturdays only a few times during the summer to be used in the wooden ice-cream freezers.

20 She took the bags from me and disappeared through the kitchen door. I looked around the room that I had never in my wildest fantasies imagined I would see. Browned photographs leered or threatened from the walls and the white, freshly done curtains pushed against themselves and against the wind. I

wanted to gobble up the room entire and take it to Bailey, who would help me analyze and enjoy it.

21   "Have a seat, Marguerite. Over there by the table." She carried a platter covered with a tea towel. Although she warned that she hadn't tried her hand at baking sweets for some time, I was certain that like everything else about her the cookies would be perfect.

22   They were flat round wafers, slightly browned on the edges and butter-yellow in the center. With the cold lemonade they were sufficient for childhood's lifelong diet. Remembering my manners, I took nice little lady-like bites off the edges. She said she had made them expressly for me and that she had a few in the kitchen that I could take home to my brother. So I jammed one whole cake in my mouth and the rough crumbs scratched the insides of my jaws, and if I hadn't had to swallow, it would have been a dream come true.

23   As I ate she began the first of what we later called "my lessons in living." She said that I must always be intolerant of ignorance but understanding of illiteracy. That some people, unable to go to school, were more educated and even more intelligent than college professors. She encouraged me to listen carefully to what country people called mother wit. That in those homely sayings was couched the collective wisdom of generations.

24   When I finished the cookies she brushed off the table and brought a thick, small book from the bookcase. I had read *A Tale of Two Cities* and found it up to my standards as a romantic novel. She opened the first page and I heard poetry for the first time in my life.

25   "It was the best of times and the worst of times. . . ." Her voice slid in and curved down through and over the words. She was nearly singing. I wanted to look at the pages. Were they the same that I had read? Or were there notes, music, lined on the pages, as in a hymn book? Her sounds began cascading gently. I knew from listening to a thousand preachers that she was nearing the end of her reading, and I hadn't really heard, heard to understand, a single word.

26   "How do you like that?"

27   It occurred to me that she expected a response. The sweet vanilla flavor was still on my tongue and her reading was a wonder in my ears. I had to speak.

28   I said, "Yes, ma'am." It was the least I could do, but it was the most also.

29 "There's one more thing. Take this book of poems and memorize one for me. Next time you pay me a visit, I want you to recite."

30 I have tried often to search behind the sophistication of years for the enchantment I so easily found in those gifts. The essence escapes but its aura remains. To be allowed, no, invited, into the private lives of strangers, and to share their joys and fears, was a chance to exchange the Southern bitter wormwood for a cup of mead with Beowulf or a hot cup of tea and milk with Oliver Twist. When I said aloud, "It is a far, far better thing that I do, than I have ever done . . ." tears of love filled my eyes at my selfishness.

31 On that first day, I ran down the hill and into the road (few cars ever came along it) and had the good sense to stop running before I reached the Store.

32 I was liked, and what a difference it made. I was respected not as Mrs. Henderson's grandchild or Bailey's sister but for just being Marguerite Johnson.

33 Childhood's logic never asks to be proved (all conclusions are absolute). I didn't question why Mrs. Flowers had singled me out for attention, nor did it occur to me that Momma might have asked her to give me a little talking to. All I cared about was that she had made tea cookies for *me* and read to *me* from her favorite book. It was enough to prove that she liked me.

EXERCISE 2 Vocabulary Highlights

Write a short definition of each word as it is used in the reading selection. (Paragraph numbers are given in parentheses.) Be prepared to use the words in your own sentences.

taut (2)
voile (2)
benign (4)
infuse (12)
valid (13)

leered (20)
cascading (25)
sophistication (30)
essence (30)
aura (30)

EXERCISE 3 Discussion and Critical Thinking

1. The narrator refers to Mrs. Bertha Flowers as an aristocrat and the blacks' "answer to the richest white woman in town" (part

of the situation). In what ways does she deserve that characterization? Is she rich?

2. What techniques (part of the struggle) does Mrs. Flowers use to encourage Marguerite to speak?

3. What does Mrs. Flowers mean by the word *educated*?

4. What does the narrator mean by "childhood's logic" (paragraph 33)?

5. What are "lessons in living" (paragraph 23)? In what way can this episode be called such a lesson?

6. Which one of the five parts of the narrative pattern—situation, conflict, struggle, outcome, meaning—is the lesson of this episode?

EXERCISE 4 Connecting the Paired Sources

1. Which author presents childhood experience in a more realistic fashion?

2. Although the experiences are both located well in the past, which one evokes a more contemporary feeling?

3. In your opinion, which selection more effectively makes the point that childhood experiences are important? Explain your answer.

Topics for Using Narration in Writing
Reading-Related Topics
"The Importance of Childhood"
1. In keeping with Lobsenz's ideas about the significance of childhood events, write about one formative event that has enhanced or haunted your life.
2. Using Lobsenz's brief narrative in paragraphs 1–6, write about a connection between what you experienced in childhood and a crisis you have faced. Explain how your childhood memory helped you deal with your adult situation.

"Liked for Myself"
3. Write about someone in your neighborhood (or in your household) who in his or her own way can be called an "aristocrat"—someone who has true class.
4. Write a paragraph or essay that defines the term *aristocrat* as the narrator does. Consider these aspects: how the person looks, how the person acts, what the person says, and how others react to the person. You may use Mrs. Flowers as an example; or you can write about someone you know, someone you have read about, or someone you have discovered through the media.
5. Write a detailed account of how someone helped you at a time when your self-esteem was low.
6. Assume the role of either the grandmother or Mrs. Flowers and give a report of the progress of your relationship with Marguerite.

26 Chapter 2 Narration: Moving Through Time

7. If you have helped or are now helping someone through a time of hardship, write an account of your involvement and the results.
8. Analyze this narrative account by discussing the factors (such as readiness and need by the narrator and compassion, understanding, and personal stature by Mrs. Flowers) that made the narrator's change possible.

Paired Sources on Childhood Revisited

9. Pick one of the following quotations from "The Importance of Childhood" and apply it to "Liked for Myself." In your discussion summarize the narrative about Maya Angelou and Mrs. Bertha Flowers. Use your own imagination and reasoning to speculate about the significance of Angelou's experience.

   - " 'There are those early memories,' " she [Willa Cather] wrote. " 'One cannot get another set; one has only those.' "
   - "We forget that, to them, childhood is reality rather than merely a preparation for reality. We forget that childhood memories form the adult personality."
   - "We [parents, adults] can give them [children] a memory of courage rather than fear; of strength rather than weakness; of an appetite for adventure rather than a shrinking from new people and places; of warmth and affection rather than rigidity and coldness."

Career-Related Topics

10. Write a narrative account of a work-related encounter between a management person and a worker and briefly explain the significance of the event.
11. Write a narrative account of an encounter between a customer and a salesperson. Explain what went right and what went wrong.
12. Write a narrative account of how a person solved a work-related problem.
13. Write a narrative account of a salesperson dealing with a customer's complaint. Critique the procedure.

General Topics

Each of the following topics concerns the writing of a narrative with meaning beyond the story itself. The narrative will be used to inform or persuade in relation to a clearly stated idea.

14. Write a narrative based on a topic sentence such as this: "One experience showed me what _____ [pain, fear, anger, love, sacrifice, dedication, joy, sorrow, shame, pride] was really like."
15. Write a simple narrative about a fire, a riot, an automobile accident, a rescue, shoplifting, or some other unusual happening you witnessed.
16. Write a narrative that supports (or opposes) the idea of a familiar saying such as one of the following:

> You never know who a friend is 'til you need one.
>
> A bird in the hand is worth two in the bush.
>
> A person who is absent is soon forgotten.
>
> Better to be alone than to be in bad company.
>
> A person in a passion rides a mad horse.
>
> Borrowing is the mother of trouble.
>
> A person who marries for money earns it.
>
> The person who lies down with dogs gets up with fleas.
>
> Never give advice to a friend.
>
> If it isn't broken, don't fix it.
>
> Nice people finish last.
>
> It's not what you know, it's whom you know.
>
> Fools and their money are soon parted.
>
> Every person has a price.
>
> You get what you pay for.
>
> Haste makes waste.
>
> The greatest remedy for anger is delay.
>
> A person full of him- or herself is empty.
>
> To forget a wrong is the best revenge.
>
> Money is honey, my little sonny,
> And a rich man's joke is always funny.

3

Description: Moving Through Space

At a Glance: Using Description in Writing

1. Description is the use of words to represent the appearance or nature of something in either an objective or a subjective manner.
2. Effective **objective description** presents the subject clearly and directly, as if it exists outside the realm of feelings.
   - For objective description—for example, a biology lab report—use direct, practical language appealing mainly to the sense of sight.
3. Effective **subjective description** is also concerned with clarity and it may be direct, but in addition it conveys a feeling about the subject and sets a mood while making a point.
   - For subjective description, appeal to the reader's feelings, especially through images of sight, sound, smell, taste, and touch.
4. Instead of using general, abstract words, consider using specific, concrete words to enhance your description.
   - *Food* is general; *Oreo cookie* is specific.
   - *Beauty* is abstract; *sunset* is concrete.
5. Apply these questions to your writing:
   - What is the dominant impression I am trying to convey?
   - What details support the dominant impression?

- What is the primary order of the details as I present them: time or place?
- What is the point of view? Am I avoiding needless shifts by using either the first-person (*I*) or the third-person (*he, she, it, they*) perspective? Am I as the writer involved in what I describe?

6. Consider giving your description a narrative framework (situation, conflict, struggle, outcome, significance).

PAIRED SOURCES ON RESTAURANTS— FOOD, SERVICE, AMBIANCE

One of the most common American experiences is eating food prepared outside the home kitchen. A surprisingly large percentage of families "outsource" (to use a contemporary term) most of their main meals. It's not surprising, therefore, that we talk a great deal about restaurants. And when we do, we're likely to talk about the nature of the food, the service, and the atmosphere of the establishment. The more elegant term *ambiance* may not seem to fit the overall impression you get at the local eatery, but that's what it is.

The paired selections offer perspectives from individuals who are traveling out of town. In "On the Road," Sue Hubbell reports on truck stops, getting beyond the road dust, garish neon signs, plastic stools, and Formica counters to focus on the hash slingers and coffee pourers of the "truckers' hours." "In the Land of 'Coke-Cola,'" William Least Heat-Moon discovers a café that balances quantity with quality in a folksy atmosphere, where he fills up on both food and hospitality.

On the Road: A City of the Mind
Sue Hubbell

As both a former trucker and a keen observer of human nature, Sue Hubbell is well qualified to analyze truck-stop culture. The all-night food-and-gas establishments she writes about cater to truckers, accept tourists as second-class citizens during daylight hours, and—in the dead of night—become a "city of the mind" for workers and drivers. These men and women are linked by common feelings, needs, and behavior. This article first appeared in Time *magazine.*

1. In the early morning there is a city of the mind that stretches from coast to coast, from border to border. Its cross streets are the interstate highways, and food, comfort, companionship are served up in its buildings, the truck stops near the exits. Its citizens are all-night drivers, the truckers and the waitresses at the stops.

2. In daylight the city fades and blurs when the transients appear, tourists who merely want a meal and a tank of gas. They file into the carpeted dining rooms away from the professional drivers' side, sit at the Formica tables set off by imitation cloth flowers in bud vases. They eat and are gone, do not return. They are not a part of the city and obscure it.

3. It is 5 A.M. in a truck stop in West Virginia. Drivers in twos, threes and fours are eating breakfast and talking routes and schedules.

4. "Truckers!" growls a manager. "They say they are in a hurry. They complain if the service isn't fast. We fix it so they can have their fuel pumped while they are eating and put in telephones on every table so they can check with their dispatchers. They could be out of here in half an hour. But what do they do? They sit and talk for two hours."

5. The truckers are lining up for seconds at the breakfast buffet (all you can eat for $3.99—biscuits with chipped-beef gravy, fruit cup, French toast with syrup, bacon, pancakes, sausage, scrambled eggs, doughnuts, Danish, cereal in little boxes).

6. The travel store at the truck stop has a machine to measure heartbeat in exchange for a quarter. There are racks of jackets, belts, truck supplies, tape cassettes. On the wall are paintings for sale, simulated wood with likenesses of John Wayne or a stag. The rack by the cash register is stuffed with Twinkies and chocolate Suzy Qs.

7. It is 5 A.M. in New Mexico. Above the horseshoe-shaped counter on panels where a menu is usually displayed, an overhead slide show is in progress. The pictures change slowly, allowing the viewer to take in all the details. A low shot of a Peterbilt, its chrome fittings sparkling in the sunshine, is followed by one of a bosomy young woman, the same who must pose for those calendars found in auto-parts stores. She almost has on clothes, and she is offering to check a trucker's oil. The next slide is a side view of a whole tractor-trailer rig, its 18 wheels gleaming and spoked. It is followed by one of a blond

Paired Sources on Restaurants—Food, Service, Ambiance

bulging out of a hint of cop clothes writing a naughty trucker a ticket.

8   The waitress looks too tired and too jaded to be offended. The jaws of the truckers move mechanically as they fork up their eggs-over-easy. They stare at the slides, glassy eyed, as intent on chrome as on flesh.

9   It is 4 A.M. in Oklahoma. A recycled Stuckey's with blue tile roof calls itself simply Truck Stop. The sign also boasts showers, scales, truck wash and a special on service for $88.50. At a table inside, four truckers have ordered a short stack and three eggs apiece, along with bacon, sausage and coffee. (Trucker's Superbreakfast—$3.79).

10 They have just started drinking their coffee, and the driver with the Roadway cap calls over the waitress, telling her there is salt in the sugar he put in his coffee. She is pale, thin, young, has dark circles under her eyes. The truckers have been teasing her, and she doesn't trust them. She dabs a bit of sugar from the canister on a finger and tastes it. Salt. She samples sugar from the other canisters. They have salt too, and she gathers them up to replace them. Someone is hazing her, breaking her into her new job. Her eyes shine with tears.

11 She brings the food and comes back when the truckers are nearly done. She carries a water jug and coffeepot on her tray. The men are ragging her again, and her hands tremble. The tray falls with a crash. The jug breaks. Glass, water and coffee spread across the floor. She sits down in the booth, tears rolling down her cheeks.

12 "I'm so tired. My old man . . . he left me," she says, the tears coming faster now. "The judge says he's going to take my kid away if I can't take care of him, so I stay up all day and just sleep when he takes a nap and the boss yells at me and . . . and . . . the truckers all talk dirty . . . I'm so tired."

13 She puts her head down on her arms and sobs luxuriantly. The truckers are gone, and I touch her arm and tell her to look at what they have left. There is a $20 bill beside each plate. She looks up, nods, wipes her eyes on her apron, pockets the tips and goes to get a broom and a mop.

14 It is 3:30 A.M. in Illinois at a glossy truck stop that offers all mechanical services, motel rooms, showers, Laundromat, game room, TV lounge, truckers' bulletin board and a stack of newspapers published by the Association of Christian Truckers. Piped-in music fills the air.

15   The waitress in the professional drivers' section is a big motherly-looking woman with red hair piled in careful curls on top of her head. She correctly sizes up the proper meal for the new customer at the counter. "Don't know what you want, honey? Try the chicken-noodle soup with a hot roll. It will stick to you like you've got something, and you don't have to worry about grease."

16   She has been waitressing 40 years, 20 of them in this truck stop. As she talks she polishes the stainless steel, fills mustard jars, adds the menu inserts for today's special (hot turkey sandwich, mashed potatoes and gravy, pot of coffee—$2.50).

17   "The big boss, well, he's a love, but some of the others aren't so hot. But it's a job. Gotta work somewhere. I need a day off though. Been working six, seven days straight lately. Got shopping to do. My lawn needs mowing."

18   Two truckers are sitting at a booth. Their faces are lined and leathery. One cap says Harley-Davidson, the other Coors.

19   Harley-Davidson calls out, "If you wasn't so mean, Flossie, you'd have a good man to take care of you and you wouldn't have to mow the damn lawn."

20   She puts down the mustard jar, walks over to Harley-Davidson and Coors, stands in front of them, hands on wide hips. "Now you listen here, Charlie, I'm good enough woman for any man but all you guys want are chippies."

21   Coors turns bright red. She glares at him. "You saw my ex in here last Saturday night with a chippie on his arm. He comes in here all the time with two, three chippies just to prove to me what a high old time he's having. If that's a good time, I'd rather baby-sit my grandkids."

22   Chippies are not a topic of conversation that Charlie and Coors wish to pursue. Coors breaks a doughnut in two, and Charlie uses his fork to make a spillway for the gravy on the double order of mashed potatoes that accompanies his scrambled eggs.

23   Flossie comes back and turns to the new customer in mirror shades at this dark hour, a young trucker with cowboy boots and hat. "John-boy. Where you been? Haven't seen you in weeks. Looks like you need a nice omelet. Cook just made some of those biscuits you like too."

24   I leave a tip for Flossie and pay my bill. In the men's room, where I am shunted because the ladies' is closed for

cleaning, someone has scrawled poignant words: NO TIME TO EAT NOW.

EXERCISE 1 Vocabulary Highlights

Write a short definition of each word as it is used in the reading selection. (Paragraph numbers are given in parentheses.) Be prepared to use the words in your own sentences.

transients (2)
Formica (2)
obscure (2)
simulated (6)
jaded (8)

canister (10)
hazing (10)
luxuriantly (13)
chippie (21)
poignant (24)

EXERCISE 2 Discussion and Critical Thinking

1. What does the subtitle "A City of the Mind" mean? How can that "city" be described?

2. Hubbell describes four locations, in no particular order. Why doesn't she place them in order according to time or distance?

3. Why do tourists eat in different sections of the truck stops?

4. How is the waitress in paragraph 10 different from the model in the picture in paragraph 7?

34 Chapter 3 Description: Moving Through Space

5. Why is Flossie (paragraphs 14–24) doing better than the waitress in Oklahoma (paragraphs 9–13)?

6. What are the two most specific food items?

7. What are other examples of very specific diction used to help the reader visualize specific items?

8. Which of the four truck stops is described with the greatest clarity?

In the Land of "Coke-Cola"
William Least Heat-Moon

William Trogdon, of English-Irish-Osage ancestry, writes under the pen name William Least Heat-Moon. Traveling around the country in the old van he called Ghost Dancing, he sought out locales on secondary highways marked in blue on road maps. A collection of his descriptions of these adventures subsequently became the best-selling book Blue Highways. *Here he visits a folksy all-you-can-eat restaurant in rural Georgia.*

1   In the land of "Coke-Cola" it was hot and dry. The artesian water was finished. Along route 72, an hour west of Ninety-Six, I tried not to look for a spring; I knew I wouldn't find one, but I kept looking. The Savannah River, dammed to an unnatural wideness, lay below, wet and cool. I'd come into Georgia. The sun seemed to press on the roadway, and inside the truck, hot light bounced off chrome, flickering like a torch. Then I saw what I was trying not to look for: in a coppice, a long-handled pump.

2   I stopped and took my bottles to the well. A small sign: WATER UNSAFE FOR DRINKING. I drooped like warm tallow. What fungicide, herbicide, nematicide, fumigant, or growth regulant—potions that rebuilt Southern agriculture—had seeped into the ground water? In the old movie Westerns there is commonly a scene where a dehydrated man, crossing the barren waste, at last comes to a water hole; he lies flat to drink the tepid stuff. Just as lips touch water, he sees on the other side a steer skull. I drove off thirsty but feeling a part of mythic history.

3   The thirst subsided when hunger took over. I hadn't eaten since morning. Sunset arrived west of Oglesby, and the air cooled. Then a roadsign:

SWAMP GUINEA'S FISH LODGE
ALL YOU CAN EAT!

An arrow pointed down a country highway. I would gorge myself. A record would be set. They'd ask me to leave. An embarrassment to all.

4   The road through the orange earth of north Georgia passed an old, three-story house with a thin black child hanging out of every window like an illustration for "The Old Woman Who Lived in a Shoe"; on into hills and finally to Swamp Guinea's, a conglomerate of plywood and two-by-fours laid over with the smell of damp pine woods.

5   Inside, wherever an oddity or natural phenomenon could hang, one hung: stuffed rump of a deer, snowshoe, flintlock, hornet's nest. The place looked as if a Boy Scout troop had decorated it. Thirty or so people, black and white, sat around tables almost foundering under piled platters of food. I took a seat by the reproduction of a seventeenth-century woodcut depicting some Rabelaisian banquet at the groaning board.

6   The diners were mostly Oglethorpe County red-dirt farmers. In Georgia tones they talked about their husbandry in terms of rain and nitrogen and hope. An immense woman with a glossy picture of a hooked bass leaping the front of her shirt said, "I'm gonna be sick from how much I've ate."

7   I was watching everyone else and didn't see the waitress standing quietly by. Her voice was deep and soft like water moving in a cavern. I ordered the $4.50 special. In a few minutes she wheeled up a cart and began offloading dinner: ham

and eggs, fried catfish, fried perch fingerlings, fried shrimp, chunks of barbecued beef, fried chicken, French fries, hush puppies, a broad bowl of cole slaw, another of lemon, a quart of ice tea, a quart of ice, and an entire loaf of factory-wrapped white bread. The table was covered.

8   "Call me if y'all want any more." She wasn't joking. I quenched the thirst and then—slowly—went to the eating. I had to stand to reach plates across the table, but I intended to do the supper in. It was all Southern fried and good, except the Southern-style sweetened ice tea; still I took care of a quart of it. As I ate, making up for meals lost, the Old-Woman-in-the-Shoe house flashed before me, lightning in darkness. I had no moral right to eat so much. But I did. Headline: STOMACH PUMP FAILS TO REVIVE TRAVELER.

9   The loaf of bread lay unopened when I finally abandoned the meal. At the register, I paid a man who looked as if he'd been chipped out of Georgia chert. The Swamp Guinea. I asked about the name. He spoke of himself in the third person like the Wizard of Oz. "The Swamp Guinea only tells regulars."

10 "I'd be one, Mr. Guinea, if I didn't live in Missouri."

11 "Y'all from the North? Here, I got somethin' for you." He went to the office and returned with a 45 rpm record. "It's my daughter singin'. A little promotion we did. Take it along." Later, I heard a husky north Georgia voice let go a down-home lyric rendering of Swamp Guinea's menu:

> *That's all you can eat*
> *For a dollar fifty,*
> *Hey! The barbecue's nifty!*

And so on through the fried chicken and potatoes.

12 As I left, the Swamp Guinea, a former antique dealer whose name was Rudell Burroughs, said, "The nickname don't mean anything. Just made it up. Tried to figure a good one so we can franchise someday."

13 The frogs, high and low, shrilled and bellowed from the trees and ponds. It was cool going into Athens, a city suffering from a nasty case of the sprawls. On the University of Georgia campus, I tried to walk down Swamp Guinea's supper. Everywhere couples entwined like moonflower vines, each waiting for the blossom that opens only once.

Paired Sources on Restaurants—Food, Service, Ambiance **37**

EXERCISE 3 Vocabulary Highlights

Write a short definition of each word as it is used in the reading selection. (Paragraph numbers are given in parentheses.) Be prepared to use the words in your own sentences.

artesian (1)
coppice (1)
fungicide (2)
herbicide (2)
nematicide (2)

fumigant (2)
dehydrated (2)
conglomerate (4)
chert (9)
entwined (13)

EXERCISE 4 Discussion and Critical Thinking

1. How many of the five senses are represented in the imagery? Give an example of each one you find.

2. What ideas dominate each section as the writer moves from one phase of his experience to another?

3. You learn a great deal about the location and the residents in this passage. What do you learn about William Least Heat-Moon by the way he describes his experience?

4. What kind of audience do you think the author anticipates? Why?

38 Chapter 3 Description: Moving Through Space

EXERCISE 5 Connecting the Paired Sources

1. Point of view is significant in each of these essays. Both are written in the first person. How much do the authors involve themselves in describing their subjects?

2. With which waitress in the Hubbell essay would you compare the waitress at Swamp Guinea's place? Of those two, whom do you get to know better?

3. Of the three principal aspects of a restaurant—food, service, ambiance—which ones are the authors most concerned with? Rank each author's concerns.

4. Which author do you get to know better?

5. Hubbell makes a case for truck stops across the country becoming a city of the mind in the late-night and early-morning hours. Does Least Heat-Moon imply that Swamp Guinea's Fish Lodge also represents people with a certain mindset in the late-afternoon and early-evening hours?

6. Drawing on your experiences, which situation do you relate to? Why?

TOPICS FOR USING DESCRIPTION IN WRITING
Reading-Related Topics
"On the Road: A City of the Mind"
1. Step outside yourself and objectively write about yourself at work. Describe the setting, people, and the objects or services being produced, sold, or developed. Decide on a dominant impression to make a statement beyond mere description.
2. Using "On the Road" as a model, describe a situation that illustrates the problems of working women. Concentrate on a single point in time, a single event.

"In the Land of 'Coke-Cola' "
3. Describe a colorful restaurant, concentrating on food, service, and ambiance. Integrate the parts of your description by presenting a scene involving someone ordering and/or eating food, or someone serving food to a customer.

Paired Sources on Restaurants—Food, Service, Ambiance
4. Compare one or more of the features—food, service, ambiance—of Swamp Guinea's place and any of the truck stops in "On the Road." Include descriptive details. Explain the significance of the differences.
5. Compare the waitress who served Least Heat-Moon with any waitress in Hubbell's essay.
6. Describe a colorful waitress you know. Show her in action, and describe some of her traits by referring to the two essays.

Career-Related Topics
7. Describe a well-furnished, well-functioning office or other work area. Be specific.
8. Describe a computer-related product; pay special attention to the dominant trait that gives the product its reputation.
9. Describe a person groomed and attired for a particular job or interview. Be specific in giving details pertaining to the person and in naming the place or situation. Describe yourself from a detached point of view if you like.

General Topics
Be sure to keep your purpose and audience in mind.

Chapter 3 Description: Moving Through Space

Objective Description

10. A visible part of your body, such as a toe, finger, ear, nose, or eye
11. A construction, such as a building, room, desk, chair, or table
12. A mechanism, such as a bicycle, wagon, car, motorcycle, CD player, can opener, or stapler

Subjective Description

13. Personalize a trip to a supermarket, stadium, airport, unusual house, mall, beach, courtroom, house of worship, club, business, library, or police or fire station. Describe a simple conflict in one of those places while emphasizing descriptive details.
14. Pick a high point in any event and describe the most important few seconds. Consider how the scene can be captured by a video camera and then give the event focus by applying the dominant-impression principle, using relevant images of sight, sound, taste, touch, and smell. The event might be a ball game, a graduation or wedding ceremony, funeral, dance, concert, family gathering, class meeting, rally, riot, robbery, fight, proposal, or meal. Limit your subject material to what you can cover effectively in the passage you write.

4

Exemplification: Writing with Examples

At a Glance: Using Exemplification in Writing

1. Use examples to explain, convince, or amuse.
2. Use examples that are vivid, specific, and representative.

   - Vivid examples (the most colorful or memorable from your list of possible examples) attract attention.
   - Specific examples (such as names of places, things, and people) are identifiable.
   - Representative examples (those that are recognizable to readers) are typical and therefore the basis for generalization.

3. Tie your examples clearly to your thesis and your main points.
4. Draw your examples from what you have read, heard, and experienced.
5. Brainstorm a list or cluster of possible examples before you write.
6. Choose the order (time, place, or emphasis) and number of your examples according to the purpose stated in your topic sentence or thesis.

PAIRED SOURCES ON LOUD TALKING

We know about property rights as they pertain to real estate, vehicles, clothing, and so on. These things are ours, and people should not mess with them without our permission. But what about space as it pertains to sound? Do you have any right to claim that

42 Chapter 4 Exemplification: Writing with Examples

> space in public places? Are you ever bothered by nearby conversations in a movie theater? Or let's say the restaurant lights are low, the music is soft, and you are staring into the misty eyes of your dream date. Suddenly a loud cell phone talker in the next booth proceeds to place a detailed order of pork belly futures to his broker. Bothered? Have you been violated? Are you just too old? In this pair of sources, Jennifer Oldham in "Amid Backlash, Calls for Cell Phone Etiquette" and James Lileks in "The Talkies" provide you with an abundance of examples to detest or dismiss.

Amid Backlash, Calls for Cell Phone Etiquette

Jennifer Oldham

A staff writer with the Los Angeles Times, *Jennifer Oldham wrote this article as one in a series on the effects of technology on society. It attracted a lot of attention from those who use cell phones and those who do not. A 1999 poll by NBC found that 28 percent of the survey group owned cell phones and 59 percent of that same group did not want to sit next to anyone using a cell phone. The members of the latter group were irritated by cell phone use only as it invaded their cone of sound, which is Oldham's chief concern in this selection.*

1   Secondhand cell phone conversations are fast replacing secondhand smoke as public enemy No. 1 in crowded venues nationwide. Once a status symbol, mobile phones have become a necessity for about 76 million Americans—in grocery stores, commuter trains, public restrooms, even at weddings. But while cell phone use in such venues has become commonplace, public acceptance has not.

2   As is the case with many new technologies that move into the mainstream, there are no social norms dictating how and where to use a mobile phone. And it shows.

3   Fed up with customers who have phones attached to their ears, restaurants, theaters, colleges, and churches have taken steps to ban mobile phone use. Those who ignore the policies face the wrath of other patrons and often are forced to conduct their conversations outside. "Whenever someone's cell phone would ring, eighteen sets of eyes would roll in their sockets," said restaurateur Danny Meyer, who has asked patrons to turn

off their mobile phones in the four eateries he co-owns in New York. "A lot of people were being downright rude and showy and talking way over the crowd." Patrons at New York's popular Union Square Cafe are greeted with signs that read, "Please 86 all cell phone use in the dining room."

4   It should hardly come as a surprise that mobile phones have become as common as day planners for busy Americans. The 76 million mobile phone users in the United States represent a 300-percent increase from the 19 million in 1994, according to the Cellular Telephone Industry Association. And the number is expected to grow 25 percent annually as more people take advantage of offers for free phones and free calling time.

5   But with the influx of any time–anywhere communication comes the inevitable backlash. Call them the mobile phone etiquette pioneers, the brave souls who have dared to suggest that being tethered to the world twenty-four hours a day might not be such a good idea. At UCLA's new law library, officials took action to silence mobile phones after conversations created a ruckus in the first-floor reading room. "During finals in May, we had so many complaints from students about cell phones that we put up a laminated sign with a big phone with a slash through it," said Karen Nikos, director of communications at the UCLA School of Law. At the Stephen S. Wise Temple in Los Angeles, rabbis decided to print an announcement at the bottom of a weekly bulletin asking worshipers not to use their phones at the synagogue.

6   But intrusive cell phone use may not be the result of cheaper technology so much as the overall demise of common courtesy in the United States. "This is one part of a larger patchwork of behavior that shows disrespect for the value of public space and public discourse and sense of community in favor of celebration of oneself," said Jim Katz, a professor of communications at Rutgers University in New Jersey and author of "Connections: Social and Cultural Studies of the Telephone in American Life."

7   Once purchased for use only in emergencies, mobile phones today are wielded in such a freewheeling manner that it's no wonder that stabs at imposing mobile phone etiquette have taken users by surprise. Whittier resident Doris Riley didn't think twice recently when she dialed her boss during breakfast at one of her favorite eateries. But she considered boycotting its rich coffee after she was kicked out of the dining room during a

call. "The owner came running at me very loud and said: 'You can't use a cell phone here. We have people eating and they want to eat in peace,'" she said. "I was really embarrassed because it's so small there. Everything went dead silent." Millie's, a hip Silver Lake hangout that Riley often visits with friends, is among a growing number of Southland restaurants that ask diners to yak outside. Owner Patti Peck says that when someone makes a call in the dining room, it's not unusual for the staff to start chanting, "No phones, no phones" and for customers to join in.

8   Ron Riddle, a resident of Dayton, Ohio, doesn't own a cell phone. But he does eat out often and is all in favor of restaurants controlling the atmosphere in their dining rooms—within limits. "Which seating preference would you like this evening, sir?" Riddle said, "Smoking or nonsmoking? Cell phone or non–cell phone? Crying babies or non–crying babies? Loudmouth drunks or non–loudmouth drunks?" Those on etiquette's front lines say they have received positive feedback about their policies. Roberto Aguilar, who manages the French restaurant Aubergine in Newport Beach, said a request on the menu—"Please no cell phones, thank you"—has prompted customers to tell him they were amazed to not hear one ring during their meal.

9   For New York restaurateur Meyer, the freshly imposed restrictions at his establishments haven't hurt business. "I have a file full of letters from people saying, 'Thank you for taking a stand.' Most people are happy to know what you expect of them," he said. "This technology has grown up so quickly that most people have not stopped to think what the etiquette should be."

EXERCISE 1   Discussion and Critical Thinking

1. Is the author objective or subjective?

2. Which is the thesis, the first or the second sentence of the essay? Notice that the third sentence echoes the thesis.

3. How many examples are used in paragraph 3?

4. How does Jim Katz, professor of communications at Rutgers University, explain the use of the cell phone?

5. Does a restriction on cell phone use seem to affect business negatively?

6. How many specific examples (by name or time) are included? Include the paragraph number for each.

7. Is this topic presented fairly? Explain.

The Talkies

James Lileks

A columnist for the Minneapolis Star Tribune *and a contributor to the* Washington Post, *James Lileks is well known for his humorous observations on human behavior. He is the author of two novels,* Falling up the Stairs *(1988) and* Mr. Obvious *(1995), and two collections of essays,* Notes of a Nervous Man *(1991) and* Fresh Lies *(1995), which contains the following selection.*

1   I am a tolerant man. Especially at the movies. I do not complain when the seats are as plush as a Baptist pew, or the buttered popcorn tastes like packing material with a drizzle of melted crayon. I don't mind that I have to cash a bond to buy a box of

Dots, and if I have to use solvents to free my feet from the floor at the end of the film, that's acceptable. I'm not happy when the man with the big yellow hat from the Curious George books sits directly in front of me and blocks my view, but accept it as the price you pay for a communal experience.

2   But people who talk in movies make me turn eight shades of mad. Plunk two talkers behind me and I start to pine for a decent billy club. Something well weighted with a comfortable grip. As I see it, there are two excuses for talking during movies: (a) you are on the screen; or (b) you have a rare neurological disease that causes you to blurt out statements like "I CAN'T BELIEVE SISKEL AND EBERT GAVE THIS TWO THUMBS UP!" at inappropriate times—and so you go to movie theaters where your affliction seems less bizarre.

3   Mind you, I am not discussing those who lean to their partner and whisper a few words or observations. Most of you whisper, or keep it to yourselves. The people to whom I refer are those who speak at a volume just a few decibels shy of the level you would use to warn someone in a crowd of a falling piano. The people who seem to expect their names to be listed in the credits under "Additional Dialogue."

4   Last week I went to see *Mississippi Burning*. I use the word "see" with precision, for I heard not a line of the dialogue. The entire row behind me talked all through the trailers. That's fine. That's what trailers are for. Go on, get it out of your system. They also talked during the opening credits, but that was acceptable; they'd arrived late—I know this because one of them hit me in the head with her purse—and they were still flush with the excitement that comes with leaving the house three minutes before the film starts.

5   But as the film progressed, it became obvious that the row behind us was a group from the Institute for Pointing Out the Obvious, off on a field trip. The first image of the film, an early '60s-model car cresting a hill, prompted the gentleman behind me to note, "That's an old car." The appearance of several more cars of the same period gave the man an empirical Epiphany, and he could not help but burst out with his conclusion:

6   "This must be set in the past."

7   There was a period of silence, during which he may or may not have whispered, "Note how reflective and rectangular the screen is," to his partner. The slack was taken up by a group to his right, who were attempting to recall what this film was

about, perhaps on the assumption that the plot, due to malicious filmmakers anxious for financial ruin, would remain inscrutable for the next two hours.

8   These folk soon shut up—after my buddy had turned around, locked eyes, and given his best I-taught-Manson-all-he-knows look. But the ones behind me were just beginning.

9   Nothing escaped comment. The streets in the rural Mississippi town were unpaved? Lo, hear them discuss the volume of dust raised by a passing car. The sheriff was fat? Lend an ear to "Looka that gut," and other biting witticisms (such as, "I mean it, how can he be that fat? I'll never get that fat."). Woe to any screen characters who fail to heed their judgments, and prolonged approval of those who do.

10 Often I was treated to a critical evaluation in process. At one point, Gene Hackman drives up to the house of a woman who knows something but isn't telling the Feds. This prompts the following speech:

11 "Oh, it's broad daylight, he'd better not go up to that house. People would talk and her husband would hear about it, don't you think?"

12 "I imagine so."

13 "Well, everyone knows that's his car."

14 "See, he's leaving."

15 "Yeah, he's turning around."

16 "Good. 'Cause he'd have gotten in trouble, and so would she."

17 Turning around and shouting "SHUT UP! SHUT UP AND REMAIN IN A STATE OF SHUTUPEDNESS!" would have done no good. I had spent the previous hour turning around and glaring, but they apparently took this to mean I was angry that they were speaking too softly, and hence depriving me of their views. For a while I was turning around, glaring and turning away with a heavy sigh, but given the classical decor of the theater, they probably interpreted this as a nostalgic sigh of regret for an idealized world long passed. Nothing worked. When the man issued a few racking coughs interspersed with words, I considered lighting up a cigarette and letting the smoke waft his way, but smoking, of course, is considered discourteous to others.

18 For a while I attempted to use telekinesis to loose a piece of plaster on the ceiling directly above them, but this did not work.

19   I finally turned around and said, "Quiet!" They nodded, as though I was describing an attribute of the theater. I might as well have said "Dark!" or "Chairs in rows!" They embarked anew on another discussion of whether or not that actor was in that Jack Nicholson film.

20   Actors, incidentally, were not allowed to have roles. When they discussed the motivations of Gene Hackman's character, they addressed him as Gene Hackman. "See, Gene Hackman wants to do it his way, that's the problem." This helped all of us within hearing range maintain our suspension of disbelief. Willem Dafoe, late of *Platoon,* was known only as "the guy in the glasses." They would occasionally bring out the depth in his character by asking, "Why is he always wearing a suit? It looks so warm, doesn't he sweat?"

21   If I seem to be exaggerating, I assure you I am not. These people babbled without cease, as though the fountain at the concession stand had added sodium pentothal to their beverages. I could not move, as there was not a decent seat to be had in the theater. I could barely concentrate on the film, as I was always steeled for another pronouncement. All I could do was entertain the idea of following them home, standing in the corner of their bedroom, and saying things like, "Oh, see, he has his arm around her shoulder, he likes her. Okay, well, she's getting ready for bed now, that's a nice set of sheets, I have ones like those at home. Say, that's quite a mole, I'd get that checked out if I had a mole like that," and so forth.

22   It would only be fair.

23   So, friends, if you're in a movie house, and you have something to say, ask yourself this: Do you, in the course of your day, constantly have to shout over the sound of a jackhammer, and should you now adjust your voice accordingly? Is what you have to say really necessary? Is the gentleman in front of you waving a flag on which is printed the nautical symbol for PUT A LID ON IT?

24   If you feel you still have to speak, ask yourself this: If this was World War II, and I was behind German lines with Nazis everywhere, could the Nazis hear me if I spoke at this level, and subsequently submit me to horrible torture? If the answer is yes, tone it down. Or write it out and hand it to your partner, with the instructions to swallow it immediately.

25   Or, go on talking. Go ahead. You paid your money. Gab it up. And make sure you kick the seat in front of you when you

cross your legs. You're only conforming to ancient tradition, after all. Movies are nothing more than modern versions of cavemen telling tales around the fire, and back then there were always a couple who talked all through the story.

26   We know this because of drawings on the walls of caves where they buried the talkers.

EXERCISE 2   Vocabulary Highlights

Write a short definition of each word as it is used in the reading selection. (Paragraph numbers are given in parentheses.) Be prepared to use the words in your own sentences.

communal (1)
neurological (2)
empirical (5)
Epiphany (5)
inscrutable (7)

decor (17)
nostalgic (17)
interspersed (17)
telekinesis (18)
sodium pentothal (21)

EXERCISE 3   Discussion and Critical Thinking

1. Is Lileks trying to inform or to persuade his readers?

2. What is his main point?

3. How is the title ironic in this context?

4. Why is it especially appropriate that Lileks uses dialogue in his examples?

50 Chapter 4 Exemplification: Writing with Examples

5. Lileks takes his examples from a single experience, one that he seems to regard as typical of bad movie days. Does his account reflect your own experiences?

6. Assuming that Lileks has had numerous similar experiences that he could have written about, why was the choice of this specific experience particularly effective?

7. Examples are used to support ideas and therefore are used with other patterns of writing. Of these forms—narration, comparison and contrast, cause and effect, definition, and argumentation—which ones are also used significantly? Which one is used to provide a basic pattern for this selection?

EXERCISE 4 Connecting the Paired Sources

1. Which writer, James Lileks or Jennifer Oldham, is more subjective? Does the author's involvement, such as including examples from personal experience, enhance or diminish the effect of the thesis in each essay?

2. Of the two types of loud talking, which one is a more serious problem with respect to creating stress in the general population?

3. Which problem can be more easily controlled? Should society even make any attempt to control these two forms of loud talking in public places?

4. What do you think of the idea of establishing, in theaters and other public places, loud zones for those who like to speak up and quiet zones for those who don't want to either talk loudly or listen to others who do?

TOPICS FOR USING EXEMPLIFICATION IN WRITING

Reading-Related Topics

"Amid Backlash, Calls for Cell Phone Etiquette"

1. If you are bothered by the use of cell phones in public places such as restaurants, stadiums, classrooms, or places of worship, develop a paper with examples taken from what you have observed.
2. Use this selection as a model for writing a paragraph or essay of exemplification based on the idea that driving and using a cell phone are not a good combination. If you do not have an abundance of examples, consider doing research in a library or on the Internet.
3. If you believe that the benefits of unrestricted use of cell phones outweigh the problems, write a paragraph or essay of exemplification in which you explain how people depend on free cell phone use for work, family, or school.

"The Talkies"

4. Using Lileks's basic idea that self-centered or ignorant persons may spoil the enjoyment of others, discuss an experience you have had in a restaurant, lecture hall (for either a special occasion or a typical class presentation), concert, sporting event, sports bar, or house of worship. Refer to some of his points for comparison and contrast.

Paired Sources on Loud Talking

5. Some social critics have argued that loud talking is just part of an accumulation of behaviors indicating the decline of civility and the loss of individuals' respect for one another. If you subscribe to that view, write your own essay on the loss of civility, referring to examples from and views of Lileks and Oldham for some of your support.

6. Some defenders of loud talkers believe that times change, technology changes, and some people change, and that people should just learn to adjust and "tune out" the loud talk. Agree or disagree with that view in an essay that includes references to the essays by Lileks and Oldham.

Career-Related Topics

Use specific examples to support one of the following statements as applied to business or work:

7. It's not what you know; it's whom you know.
8. Don't burn your bridges.
9. Like Lego, business is a matter of connections.
10. Tact is the lubricant that oils the wheels of industry.
11. The customer is always right.
12. Money is honey, my little sonny, and a rich man's joke is always funny.
13. If you take care of the pennies, the dollars will take care of themselves.
14. A kind word turns away wrath.

General Topics

Make a judgmental statement about an issue you believe in strongly and then use one or more examples to illustrate your point. These are some possible topics:

15. The price of groceries is too high.
16. Professional athletes are paid too much.
17. A person buying a new car may get a lemon.
18. Drivers sometimes openly ignore the laws on a selective basis.
19. Politicians should be watched.
20. Working and going to school is tough.
21. Working, parenting, and going to school is tough.
22. All computer viruses have common features.
23. Many people under the age of eighteen spend too much time playing computer games.
24. Some computer games teach children useful skills.

5

Analysis by Division: Examining the Parts

At a Glance: Using Analysis by Division in Writing

Almost anything can be analyzed by division—for example, how the parts of the ear work in hearing, how the parts of the eye work in seeing, or how the parts of the heart work in pumping blood throughout the body. Subjects such as these are all approached with the same systematic procedure.

1. This is the procedure.
   - Step 1: Begin with something that is a unit.
   - Step 2: State the principle by which that unit functions.
   - Step 3: Divide the unit into parts according to the principle.
   - Step 4: Discuss each of the parts in relation to the unit.

2. This is the way you might apply that procedure to a good boss.
   - Unit: Manager
   - Principle of function: Effective as a leader
   - Parts based on the principle: Fair, intelligent, stable, competent in field
   - Discussion: Consider each part in relation to the person's effectiveness as a manager.

3. This is how a basic outline of analysis by division might look.

    Thesis: To be effective as a leader, a manager needs specific qualities.
      I. Fair
     II. Intelligent

54 Chapter 5 *Analysis by Division: Examining the Parts*

III. Stable
IV. Competent in field

> **PAIRED SOURCES ON WHAT WE ARE—
> HERITAGE AS HYPHENATION**
>
> We are all individuals, unique and separate, but we are also very much connected to those who went before us and to those who surround us. Therefore, we are all pluralistic because we have been shaped by many individuals of different cultures. Increasingly, American society is multicultural, a condition that can be traced especially to intermarriage and immigration. In response to the question "What are you?" some would answer merely "American," but others would mention the parts of their heritage. The length of the hyphenated phrase will depend on the number of contributing factors an individual wishes to include. The term may be as long as Chinese-Irish-German-American-Woman-Buddhist-Protestant-Catholic.
>
> In this pair of essays, two authors address the issue of multiple parts of self. Kesaya Noda says in "Growing Up Asian in America" that she is a Japanese, a Japanese-American, and a Japanese-American woman, although her humanity transcends all designations. In "Intermarried . . . with Children," Jill Smolowe concentrates on a broader study of the blending of cultures in America through mixed marriages and the offspring of mixed marriages, focusing on historical developments and recent trends.

Growing Up Asian in America
Kesaya E. Noda

Who are you? Can you classify yourself with a single word? Kesaya E. Noda has grown up Asian in America, but she needs several words to characterize herself because her identity has many facets.

1   Sometimes when I was growing up, my identity seemed to hurtle toward me and paste itself right to my face. I felt that way, encountering the stereotypes of my race perpetuated by non-Japanese people (primarily white) who may or may not have had contact with other Japanese in America. "You don't like cheese, do you?" someone would ask. "I know your people don't like

cheese." Sometimes questions came making allusions to history. That was another aspect of the identity. Events that had happened quite apart from the me who stood silent in that moment connected my face with an incomprehensible past. "Your parents were in California? Were they in those camps during the war?" And sometimes there were phrases or nicknames: "Lotus Blossom." I was sometimes addressed or referred to as racially Japanese, sometimes as Japanese-American, and sometimes as an Asian woman. Confusions and distortions abounded.

2 How is one to know and define oneself? From the inside—within a context that is self-defined from a grounding in community and a connection with culture and history that are comfortably accepted? Or from the outside—in terms of messages received from the media and people who are often ignorant? Even as an adult I can still see two sides of my face and past. I can see from the inside out, in freedom. And I can see from the outside in, driven by the old voices of childhood and lost in anger and fear.

I Am Racially Japanese

3 A voice from my childhood says: "You are other. You are less than. You are unalterably alien." This voice has its own history. We have indeed been seen as other and alien since the early years of our arrival in the United States. The very first immigrants were welcomed and sought as laborers to replace the dwindling numbers of Chinese, whose influx had been cut off by the Chinese Exclusion Act of 1882. The Japanese fell natural heir to the same anti-Asian prejudice that had arisen against the Chinese. As soon as they began striking for better wages, they were no longer welcomed.

4 I can see myself today as a person historically defined by law and custom as being forever alien. Being neither "free white," nor "African," our people in California were deemed "aliens, ineligible for citizenship," no matter how long they intended to stay here. Aliens ineligible for citizenship were prohibited from owning, buying, or leasing land. They did not and could not belong here. The voice in me remembers that I am always a *Japanese*-American in the eyes of many. A third-generation German-American is an American. A third-generation Japanese-American is a Japanese-American. Being Japanese

means being a danger to the country during the war and knowing how to use chopsticks. I wear this history on my face.

5   I move to the other side. I see a different light and claim a different context. My race is a line that stretches across ocean and time to link me to the shrine where my grandmother was raised. Two high, white banners lift in the wind at the top of the stone steps leading to the shrine. It is time for the summer festival. Black characters are written against the sky as boldly as the clouds, as lightly as kites, as sharply as the big black crows I used to see above the fields in New Hampshire. At festival time there is liquor and food, ritual, discipline, and abandonment. There is music and drunkenness and invocation. There is hope. Another season has come. Another season has gone.

6   I am racially Japanese. I have a certain claim to this crazy place where the prayers intoned by a neighboring Shinto priest (standing in for my grandmother's nephew who is sick) are drowned out by the rehearsals for the pop singing contest in which most of the villagers will compete later that night. The village elders, the priest, and I stand respectfully upon the immaculate, shining wooden floor of the outer shrine, bowing our heads before the hidden powers. During the patchy intervals when I can hear him, I notice the priest has a stutter. His voice flutters up to my ears only occasionally because two men and a woman are singing gustily into a microphone in the compound, testing the sound system. A prerecorded tape of guitars, samisens, and drums accompanies them. Rock music and Shinto prayers. That night, to loud applause and cheers, a young man is given the award for the most *netsuretsu*—passionate, burning—rendition of a song. We roar our approval of the reward. Never mind that his voice had wandered and slid, now slightly above, now slightly below the given line of the melody. Netsuretsu. Netsuretsu.

7   In the morning, my grandmother's sister kneels at the foot of the stone stairs to offer her morning prayers. She is too crippled to climb the stairs, so each morning she kneels here upon the path. She shuts her eyes for a few seconds, her motions as matter of fact as when she washes rice. I linger longer than she does, so reluctant to leave, savoring the connection I feel with my grandmother in America, the past, and the power that lives and shines in the morning sun.

8   Our family has served this shrine for generations. The family's need to protect this claim to identity and place out-

weighs any individual claim to any individual hope. I am Japanese.

I Am a Japanese-American

9   "Weak." I hear the voice from my childhood years. "Passive," I hear. Our parents and grandparents were the ones who were put into those camps. They went without resistance, they offered cooperation as proof of loyalty to America. "Victim," I hear. And, "Silent."

10   Our parents are painted as hard workers who were socially uncomfortable and had difficulty expressing even the smallest opinion. Clean, quiet, motivated, and determined to match the American way; that is us, and that is the story of our time here.

11   "Why did you go into those camps?" I raged at my parents, frightened by my own inner silence and timidity. "Why didn't you do anything to resist? Why didn't you name it the injustice it was?" Couldn't our parents even think? Couldn't they? Why were we so passive?

12   I shift my vision and my stance. I am in California. My uncle is in the midst of the sweet potato harvest. He is pressed, trying to get the harvesting crews onto the field as quickly as possible, worried about the flow of equipment and people. His big pickup is pulled off to the side, motor running, door ajar. I see two tractors in the yard in front of an old shed; the flatbed harvesting platform on which the workers will stand has already been brought over from the other field. It's early morning. The workers stand loosely grouped and at ease, but my uncle looks as harried and tense as a police officer trying to unsnarl a New York City traffic jam. Driving toward the shed, I pull my car off the road to make way for an approaching tractor. The front wheels of the car sink luxuriously into the soft, white sand by the roadside and the car slides to a dreamy halt, tail still on the road. I try to move forward. I try to move back. The front bites contentedly into the sand, the back lifts itself at a jaunty angle. My uncle sees me and storms down the road, running. He is shouting before he is even near me.

13   "What's the matter with you?" he screams. "What the hell are you doing?" In his frenzy, he grabs his hat off his head and slashes it through the air across his knee. He is beside himself. "Don't you know how to drive in sand? What's the matter with

you? You've blocked the whole roadway. How am I supposed to get my tractors out of here? Can't you use your head? You've cut off the whole roadway, and we've got to get out of here."

14 I stand on the road before him helplessly thinking, "No, I don't know how to drive in sand. I've never driven in sand."

15 "I'm sorry, uncle," I say, burying a smile beneath a look of sincere apology. I notice my deep amusement and my affection for him with great curiosity. I am usually devastated by anger. Not this time.

16 During the several years that follow I learn about the people and the place, and much more about what has happened in this California village where my parents grew up. The issei, or grandparents, made this settlement in the desert. Their first crops were eaten by rabbits and ravaged by insects. The land was so barren that men walking from house to house sometimes got lost. Women came here too. They bore children in 114-degree heat, then carried the babies with them into the fields to nurse when they reached the end of each row of grapes or other truck-farm crops.

17 I had no idea what it meant to buy this kind of land and make it grow green. Or how, when the war came, there was no space at all for the subtlety of being who we were—Japanese-Americans. Either/or was the way. I hadn't understood that people were literally afraid for their lives then, that their money had been frozen in banks; that there was a five-mile travel limit; that when the early evening curfew came and they were inside their houses, some of them watched helplessly as people they knew went into their barns to steal their belongings. The police were patrolling the road, interested only in violators of curfew. There was no help for them in the face of thievery. I had not been able to imagine before what it must have felt like to be an American—to know absolutely that one is an American—and yet to have almost everyone else deny it. Not only deny it, but challenge that identity with machine guns and troops of white American soldiers. In those circumstances it was difficult to say, "I'm Japanese-American." "American" had to do.

18 But now I can say that I am a Japanese-American. It means I have a place here in this country, too. I have a place here on the East Coast, where our neighbor is so much a part of our family that my mother never passes her house at night without glancing at the lights to see if she is home and safe; where my parents have hauled hundreds of pounds of rocks from fields and ardu-

ously planted Christmas trees and blueberries, lilacs, asparagus, and crab apples, where my father still dreams of angling a stream to a new bed so that he can dig a pond in the field and fill it with water and fish. "The neighbors already came for their Christmas tree?" he asks in December. "Did they like it? Did they like it?"

19   I have a place on the West Coast where my relatives still farm, where I heard the stories of feuds and backbiting, and where I saw that people survived and flourished because fundamentally they trusted and relied upon one another. A death in the family is not just a death in a family; it is a death in the community. I saw people help each other with money, materials, labor, attention, and time. I saw men gather once a year, without fail, to clean the grounds of a ninety-year-old woman who had helped the community before, during, and after the war. I saw her remembering them with birthday cards sent to each of their children.

20   I come from a people with a long memory and a distinctive grace. We live our thanks. And we are Americans. Japanese-Americans.

I Am a Japanese-American Woman

21   Woman. The last piece of my identity. It has been easier by far for me to know myself in Japan and to see my place in America than it has been to accept my line of connection with my own mother. She was my dark self, a figure in whom I thought I saw all that I feared most in myself. Growing into womanhood and looking for some model of strength, I turned away from her. Of course, I could not find what I sought. I was looking for a black feminist or a white feminist. My mother is neither white nor black.

22   My mother is a woman who speaks with her life as much as with her tongue. I think of her with her own mother. Grandmother had Parkinson's disease and it had frozen her gait and set her fingers, tongue, and feet jerking and trembling in a terrible dance. My aunts and uncles wanted her to be able to live in her own home. They fed her, bathed her, dressed her, awoke at midnight to take her for one last trip to the bathroom. My aunts (her daughters-in-law) did most of the care, but my mother went from New Hampshire to California each summer to spend a month living with Grandmother, because she wanted to and

because she wanted to give my aunts at least a small rest. During those hot summer days, mother lay on the couch watching the television or reading, cooking foods that Grandmother liked, and speaking little. Grandmother thrived under her care.

23   The time finally came when it was too dangerous for Grandmother to live alone. My relatives kept finding her on the floor beside her bed when they went to wake her in the mornings. My mother flew to California to help clean the house and make arrangements for Grandmother to enter a local nursing home. On her last day at home, while Grandmother was sitting in her big, overstuffed armchair, hair combed and wearing a green summer dress, my mother went to her and knelt at her feet. "Here, Mamma," she said. "I've polished your shoes." She lifted Grandmother's legs and helped her into the shiny black shoes. My Grandmother looked down and smiled slightly. She left her house walking, supported by her children, carrying her pocketbook, and wearing her polished black shoes. "Look, Mamma," my mom had said, kneeling. "I've polished your shoes."

24   Just the other day, my mother came to Boston to visit. She had recently lost a lot of weight and was pleased with her new shape and her feeling of good health. "Look at me, Kes," she exclaimed, turning toward me, front and back, as naked as the day she was born. I saw her small breasts and the wide, brown scar, belly button to pubic hair, that marked her because my brother and I were both born by Caesarean section. Her hips were small. I was not a large baby, but there was so little room for me in her that when she was carrying me she could not even begin to bend over toward the floor. She hated it, she said.

25   "Don't I look good? Don't you think I look good?"

26   I looked at my mother, smiling and as happy as she, thinking of all the times I have seen her naked. I have seen both my parents naked throughout my life, as they have seen me. From childhood through adulthood we've had our naked moments, sharing baths, idle conversations picked up as we moved between showers and closets, hurried moments at the beginning of days, quiet moments at the end of days.

27   I know this to be Japanese, this ease with the physical, and it makes me think of an old Japanese folk song. A young nursemaid, a fifteen-year-old girl, is singing a lullaby to a baby who is strapped to her back. The nursemaid has been sent as a servant to a place far from her own home. "We're the beggars," she says,

"and they are the nice people. Nice people wear fine sashes. Nice clothes."

> *If I should drop dead,*
> *bury me by the roadside!*
> *I'll give a flower*
> *to everyone who passes.*
>
> *What kind of flower?*
> *The cam-cam-camellia [tsun-tsun-tsubaki]*
> *watered by Heaven:*
> *alms water.*

28   The nursemaid is the intersection of heaven and earth, the intersection of the human, the natural world, the body, and the soul. In this song, with clear eyes, she looks steadily at life, which is sometimes so very terrible and sad. I think of her while looking at my mother, who is standing on the red and purple carpet before me, laughing, without any clothes.

29   I am my mother's daughter. And I am myself.

30   I am a Japanese-American woman.

Epilogue

31   I recently heard a man from West Africa share some memories of his childhood. He was raised Muslim, but when he was a young man, he found himself deeply drawn to Christianity. He struggled against his inner impulse for years, trying to avoid the church yet feeling pushed to return to it again and again. "I would have done *anything* to avoid the change," he said. At last, he became Christian. Afterwards he was afraid to go home, fearing that he would not be accepted. The fear was groundless, he discovered, when at last he returned—he had separated himself, but his family and friends (all Muslim) had not separated themselves from him.

32   The man, who is now a professor of religion, said that in the Africa he knew as a child and a young man, pluralism was embraced rather than feared. There was "a kind of tolerance that did not deny your particularity," he said. He alluded to zestful, spontaneous debates that would sometimes loudly erupt between Muslims and Christians in the village's public spaces. His memories of an atheist who harangued the villagers when he came to visit them once a week moved me deeply. Perhaps the man was

an agricultural advisor or inspector. He harassed the women. He would say: "Don't go to the fields! Don't even bother to go to the fields. Let God take care of you. He'll send you the food. If you believe in God, why do you need to work? You don't need to work! Let God put the seeds in the ground. Stay home."

33 The professor said, "The women laughed, you know? They just laughed. Their attitude was, 'Here is a child of God. When will he come home?' "

34 The storyteller, the professor of religion, smiled a most fantastic tender smile as he told this story. "In my country, there is a deep affirmation of the oneness of God," he said. "The atheist and the women were having quite different experiences in their encounter, though the atheist did not know this. He saw himself as quite separate from the women. But the women did not see themselves as being separate from him. 'Here is a child of God,' they said. 'When will he come home?' "

EXERCISE 1 Vocabulary Highlights

Write a short definition of each word as it is used in the reading selection. (Paragraph numbers are given in parentheses.) Be prepared to use the words in your own sentences.

perpetuated (1)
devastated (15)
arduously (18)
gait (22)
pluralism (32)

spontaneous (32)
harangued (32)
harassed (32)
affirmation (34)
encounter (34)

EXERCISE 2 Discussion and Critical Thinking

1. What is the unit?

2. What is the principle by which the unit is divided?

3. What are the parts of the unit?

4. What does Noda say about the people who stereotyped her?

5. What are some of the characteristics of the stereotyping she encountered?

6. Simply, what does it mean to the author to say she is Japanese-American (paragraph 18)?

7. As a Japanese-American woman, what is her legacy? What values are passed down in her family?

8. What is the significance of Noda's story about the nursemaid (paragraphs 27 and 28)?

9. Why does the author end with an epilogue about the African professor of religion?

Intermarried . . . with Children
Jill Smolowe

> In a special issue of Time *magazine, the cover image is what appears to be a photograph of an attractive young woman. The caption says, "Take a good look at this woman. She was created by a computer from a mix of several races. What you see is a remarkable preview of . . . The New Face of America: How Immigrants Are Shaping the World's First Multicultural Society." Inside, among numerous articles on cultural diversity in the United States, is this essay by Jill Smolowe. Using supporting material from reporters from Chicago, New York, and Los Angeles, she writes of the significance of the mixing of race, culture, and faith in marriage and child rearing.*

1   Hostile stares and epithets were the least of their problems when Edgar and Jean Cahn first dated. Twice the couple—he a white Jew, she a black Baptist—were arrested simply for walking the streets of Baltimore arm in arm. When they wed in 1957, Maryland law barred interracial marriages, so the ceremony was held in New York City. Although Jean had converted by then, the only rabbi who would agree to officiate denied them a huppah and the traditional breaking of glass. As law students at Yale in the 1960s, the couple lived in a basement because no landlord would rent them a flat.

2   In 1963 the Cahns moved to Washington, D.C., where they raised two sons, Reuben and Jonathan. By 1971, as co-deans of the Antioch School of Law, the high profile couple had received so many death threats that they needed bodyguards. The boys' mixed ancestry caused near riots at their public school. One principal said they "brought a dark force to the school" and called for their expulsion.

3   Now the generational wheel has turned. In 1990 young Reuben married Marna, a white Lutheran from rural Pine Grove, Pennsylvania. Although both a rabbi and a minister officiated, none of Marna's relatives, except her mother, attended the wedding. Her father fumed, "I can't believe you expect me to accept a black person, and a Jewish one at that!" But with the birth last year of towheaded Aaron, Marna's family softened considerably.

4   Intermarriage, of course, is as old as the Bible. But during the past two decades, America has produced the greatest variety of hybrid households in the history of the world. As ever in-

creasing numbers of couples crash through racial, ethnic and religious barriers to invent a life together, Americans are being forced to rethink and redefine themselves. For all the divisive talk of cultural separatism and resurgent ethnic pride, never before has a society struggled so hard to fuse such a jumble of traditions, beliefs and values.

5   The huddled masses have already given way to the muddled masses. "Marriage is the main assimilator," says Karen Stephenson, an anthropologist at UCLA. "If you really want to affect change, it's through marriage and child rearing." This is not assimilation in the Eurocentric sense of the word: one nation, under white, Anglo-Saxon Protestant rule, divided, with liberty and justice for some. Rather it is an extended hyphenation. If, say, the daughter of Japanese and Filipino parents marries the son of German and Irish immigrants, together they may beget a Japanese-Filipino-German-Irish-Buddhist-Catholic-American child. "Assimilation never really happens," says Stephenson. "Over time you get a bunch of little assimilations."

6   The profusion of couples breaching once impregnable barriers of color, ethnicity and faith is startling. Over a period of roughly two decades, the number of interracial marriages in the U.S. has escalated from 310,000 to more than 1.1 million; 72% of those polled by *Time* know married couples who are of different races. The incidence of births of mixed-race babies has multiplied 26 times as fast as that of any other group. Among Jews the number marrying out of their faith has shot up from 10% to 52% since 1960. Among Japanese Americans, 65% marry people who have no Japanese heritage; Native Americans have nudged that number to 70%. In both groups the incidence of children sired by mixed couples exceeds the number born into uni-ethnic homes.

7   Some critics fret that all this criss-crossing will damage society's essential "American" core. By this they usually mean a confluence of attitudes, values and assumptions that drive Americans' centuries-old quest for a better life. What they fail to acknowledge is that legal, educational and economic changes continuously alter the priorities within that same set of social variables. A few generations back, religion, race and custom superseded all other considerations. When Kathleen Hobson and Atul Gawande, both 27, married last year, however, they based their vision of a shared future on a different set of common values: an upper-middle-class upbringing in tightknit families, a Stanford education and a love of intellectual pursuits.

8   Unlike many other mixed couples, Gawande, an Indian American, and Hobson, a white Episcopalian of old Southern stock, have always enjoyed a warm reception from both sets of parents. Still, when Hobson first visited the Gawandes in Ohio, not every one of their friends was ready to celebrate. "One Indian family didn't want to come because they were concerned about their children being influenced," Hobson says. Their wedding in Virginia was a harmonious blend of two cultures: although Kathleen wore a white gown and her minister officiated, the ceremony included readings from both Hindu and Christian texts.

9   Tortured solutions to mixed-marriage ceremonies are common. Weddings, like funerals, are a time when family resentments, disappointments and expectations bubble to the surface. The tugging and tussling over matters that may seem frivolous set the stage for a couple's lifelong quest to create an environment that will be welcoming to both families, yet uniquely their own.

10 Accommodation and compromise only begin at the altar. The qualities that attracted Dan Kalmanson, an Anglo of European extraction, to Yilva Martinez in a Miami reggae club—her Spanish accent, exotic style of dance, and playfulness—had a more challenging echo in their married life. After they wed in 1988, Ignacio, Yilva's then eight-year-old son by a previous marriage, moved from Venezuela to join the couple. Dan, 33, spoke no Spanish, the boy no English. The couple decided to compel Ignacio to speak English. He caught on so fast that his Spanish soon degenerated. Says Yilva: "We have literally forced him to learn Spanish again."

11 For Yilva, 35, the struggle is not just to preserve her native tongue; she also wants to suffuse her home, which has grown with the addition of Kristen, 3, with the Latin ethic that values family above all else. "Here, you live to work. There, we work to live," she says. "In Venezuela we take a two-hour lunch break; we don't cram in a hamburger at McDonald's."

12 Children also force mixed couples to confront hard decisions about religion. Blanche Speiser, 43, was certain that Mark, 40, would yield if she wanted to raise their two kids Christian, but she also knew that her Jewish husband would never attend church with the family or participate in holiday celebrations. After much soul searching, she opted for a Jewish upbringing. "I knew it would be O.K. as long as the children had some belief,"

she says. "I didn't want a mishmash." Although Blanche remains comfortable with that decision and has grown accustomed to attending synagogue with her family, she admits that it pricks when Brad, 7, says, "Mommy, I wish you were Jewish." Other couples expose their families to both religions, then leave the choice to the kids.

13   When it comes to racial identity, many couples feel that a child should never have to "choose" between parents. The 1990 U.S. census form, with its "Black," "White" and "Other" boxes, particularly grated. " 'Other' is not acceptable, pure and simple," says Nancy Brown, 40. "It is psychologically damaging to force somebody to choose one identity when physiologically and biologically they are more than one." Nancy, who is white, thinks the census form should include a "Multiracial" box for her two daughters; her black husband Roosevelt, 44, argues that there should be no race box at all. Both agree that people should be able to celebrate all parts of their heritage without conflict. "It's like an equation," says Nancy, who is president of an interracial family support group. "Interracial marriage that works equals multiracial children at ease with their mixed identity, which equals more people in the world who can deal with this diversity."

14   The world still has much to learn about living with diversity. "What people say, what people do and what they say they do are three entirely different things," says anthropologist Stephenson. "We are walking contradictions." Kyoung-Hi Song, 27, was born in Korea but lived much of her youth abroad as her father was posted from one United Nations assignment to the next. Despite that cosmopolitan upbringing, her parents balked when Kyoung-Hi married Robert Dickson, a WASP from Connecticut. They boycotted the 1990 wedding, and have not contacted their daughter since. The Dicksons hope that the birth of their first child, expected in April, will change that.

15   Intolerance need not be that blatant to inflict wounds. If Tony Jeffreys, 34, and Alice Sakuda Flores, 28, have a child, that hypothetical Japanese-Filipino-German-Irish-Buddhist-Catholic-American will become flesh and blood. In their one year of marriage, Tony says, "I've heard friends say stupid stuff about Asians right in front of Alice. It is really hypocritical because a lot of them have Mexican or black girlfriends or wives." Sometimes the more subtle the rejection, the sharper the sting. Says Candy Mills, 29, the daughter of black and Native Ameri-

can parents, who is married to Gabe Grosz, a white European immigrant: "I know that people are tolerating me, not accepting me."

16 Such pain is evidence that America has yet to harvest the full rewards of its founding principles. The land of immigrants may be giving way to a land of hyphenations, but the hyphen still divides even as it compounds. Those who intermarry have perhaps the strongest sense of what it will take to return America to an unhyphenated whole. "It's American culture that we all share," says Mills. "We should capitalize on that." Perhaps her two Native American-black-white-Hungarian-French-Catholic-Jewish-American children will lead the way.

EXERCISE 3   Vocabulary Highlights

Write a short definition of each word as it is used in the reading selection. (Paragraph numbers are given in parentheses.) Be prepared to use the words in your own sentences.

epithets (1)
towheaded (3)
resurgent (4)
profusion (6)
confluence (7)

frivolous (9)
exotic (10)
degenerated (10)
suffuse (11)
boycotted (14)

EXERCISE 4   Discussion and Critical Thinking

1. In what way is the hyphenation discussed in this essay another way of saying "analysis by division"?

2. How does the marriage of Marna and Reuben illustrate both the change and lack of change in interracial marriages?

3. What is anthropologist Karen Stephenson's view of assimilation?

4. What is a mixed marriage?

5. What role do common values have in mate selection (paragraph 7)?

6. What are two common solutions to the issue of mixed-faith marriages and child rearing? Which do you think is better? Why?

7. Explain this statement: "The land of immigrants may be giving way to a land of hyphenations, but the hyphen still divides even as it compounds."

EXERCISE 5 Connecting the Paired Sources

1. Both Noda and Smolowe are concerned with hyphenation. Why is Noda's system less complicated?

2. Is Noda at odds with Smolowe, or are her views essentially consistent with Smolowe's?

3. In saying that she is a Japanese-American woman, Noda expresses concern about gender. Why doesn't Smolowe bring up that issue?

4. What does each author say about prejudice and stereotyping?

5. What solution does each author have for relieving the hostility among different groups?

6. Which author has made a deeper impression on your thinking? Why?

TOPICS FOR USING ANALYSIS BY DIVISION IN WRITING

Reading-Related Topics

"Growing Up Asian in America"

1. Write an analysis by division in which you discuss your own or someone else's origin. *Origin* here may mean ethnic group, class, or region (part of the country such as South, Midwest, East).
2. Using this essay as a model, write about who you are and why by referring to your parents and grandparents. How are they different from one another and from yourself? More important, what have you learned or inherited from them?

"Intermarried . . . with Children"

3. Write an analysis by division about the mixing of different factors in a family (for example, race, culture, faith, values, gender, generation) that have worked together but are still separate.

4. If you are a first-generation American, analyze what values or behaviors you have adopted from your contacts with American schooling and society.
5. Analyze a mixed marriage in which at least three other factors (such as education, values, interests) were more important than race, culture, or religion.
6. Considering your parents, grandparents, and any others who have significantly influenced you, give yourself a hyphenated designation and write an analysis by division about what each has contributed to you as a person. You may even include regional differences (North, South, West, East, Midwest) or different societies (country, city, inner city, suburbia).

Paired Sources on What We Are—Heritage as Hyphenation

7. Write about your own cultural makeup by discussing your hyphenated status and referring to one or both of the essays for insights or support. The hyphenation need not be exotic. It could be as simple as "Hill Country Texas-Chicago-Irish-Native American-Protestant-Free Thinker."

Career-Related Topics

8. Explain how the parts of a product function together as a unit.
9. Explain how each of several qualities of a specific person—such as his or her intelligence, sincerity, knowledgeability, ability to communicate, manner, attitude, and appearance—makes that individual an effective salesperson, manager, or employee.
10. Explain how the demands or requirements for a particular job represent a comprehensive picture of that job.
11. Explain how the aspects of a particular service (such as friendly, competent, punctual, confidential) work together in a satisfactory manner.

General Topics

Some of the following topics are too broad for a short writing assignment and should be narrowed. For example, the general "a wedding ceremony" could be narrowed to the particular: "José and María's wedding ceremony." Your focused topic should then be divided into parts and analyzed.

12. A machine such as an automobile, a computer, a camera
13. A city administration, a governmental agency, a school board, a student council

14. A wedding, graduation, or religious ceremony
15. A holiday celebration, a pep rally, a sales convention, a religious revival
16. An offensive team in football (any team in any game)
17. A family, a relationship, a gang, a club, a sorority, a fraternity
18. An album, a performance, a song, a singer, an actor, a musical group, a musical instrument
19. A movie, a television program, a video game
20. Any well-known person—athlete, politician, criminal, writer

6

Classification: Establishing Groups

At a Glance: Using Classification in Writing

1. Follow this procedure for writing paragraphs and essays of classification:
   - Select a plural subject.

     EXAMPLE: neighbors
   - Decide on a principle for grouping the units of your subject.

     EXAMPLE: involvement in neighborhood
   - Establish the groups, or classes.

     EXAMPLE: I. Friendly
              II. Meddlesome
             III. Private
2. Avoid uninteresting phrases for your classes, such as good/average/bad, fast/medium/slow, and beautiful/ordinary/ugly.
3. Avoid overlapping classes.

     EXAMPLE: I. Friendly
              II. Meddlesome
             III. Private
              IV. Wealthy (Any of the first three could be wealthy.)
4. The Roman numeral parts of your outline will probably indicate your classes.

5. If you use subclasses, clearly indicate the different levels.

   EXAMPLE: I. Friendly
            II. Meddlesome
           III. Private
                A. Shy
                B. Smug
                C. Strange

6. Following your outline, give somewhat equal (however much is appropriate) space to each class.

PAIRED SOURCES ON WAYS OF CONTROLLING

Some would argue that the greatest motivator in society, even stronger than the desire to produce offspring or make money, is the drive to control. We all know that the person with the TV remote control is the one with power; and we would all like to be the one holding that little zapper. Unfortunately, after the television set is cold and the remote is at rest, the urge to control persists.

The paired essays in this chapter deal with those who control, or at least seek control—the bosses and the naggers. In "Why We Carp and Harp," Mary Ann Hogan examines the struggle for control carried on by naggers—whether friendly, social, professional, or domestic. Naturally, naggers say all they want to do is make people better. At work, controllers are called *bosses*, and our awareness is sharpened when bosses are "bad bosses." According to some psychologists, the bad news is that all bosses are bad in certain ways. In "How to Deal with a Difficult Boss," Donna Brown Hogarty concentrates on five kinds of bad bosses: the bully, the workaholic, the jellyfish, the perfectionist, and the aloof boss—all exerting control but having trouble with it.

Why We Carp and Harp
Mary Ann Hogan

Nag. Nag. Nag. Stop! Stop! Stop! We know nagging, don't we? After all, we've heard so much of it that we're experts, right? Maybe not. Listen to what this expert says about types of naggers. She points out that in this sophisticated world, some people specialize in certain kinds of nagging. This article was first published in the Los Angeles Times.

1   Bring those dishes down from your room! Put those scissors away. . . . I told you not to smoke in the kitchen and you shouldn't be smoking anyway! Take your feet off the table! Why do I have to tell you again and again! . . . ? The hills are alive with the sound of nagging—the gnawing, crescendoing timbre of people getting in each other's face. Parents nag children, wives nag husbands, husbands nag wives, friends nag friends . . . "*Use* your fork . . . *Stop* spending money like water . . . *Can't* you be ready on time? . . . *Act* like an adult. . . ." Nagging, of course, has been around since the first cave husband refused to take out the cave garbage. But linguists, psychologists, and other scholars are just now piecing together what nagging really is, why we do it, and how to stop it before we nag each other to death.

2   Common perception holds that a nag is an unreasonably demanding wife who carps at a long-suffering husband. But in truth, nagging is universal. It happens in romances, in families, in businesses, in society—wherever people gather and one person wants another to do something he or she doesn't want to do. "It's a virus. You pick it up through kissing, shaking hands and standing in crowded rooms with people who have perfect children, wonderful husbands and sterilized homes," says humor columnist Erma Bombeck, whose family members nag her as artfully as she nags them. "It makes you feel good—like you're getting something done. Most of us want perfection in this world," she adds.

3   Thus, doctors can nag patients to lose their potbellies; accountants can nag timid clients to buy low; bosses can nag workers to get things done on time; special interest groups can nag the public to save the planet and send money; and the government can nag everyone to pay their taxes on time, to abstain from drink if they're pregnant, and, while they're at it, to Buy American. And when the going gets desperate, the desperate get nagging: Our recession-plagued nation, experts say, could be headed for a giant nag jag.

4   "When people are generally dissatisfied, they tend to harp at other people more," says Bernard Zilbergeld, a Bay Area psychologist. Naggers tend to fall into four categories—friendly, professional, social, and domestic—that range from the socially acceptable to the toxic.

5   The Friendly Ones are proud of their art. "My sisters call me a nag, but that's not necessarily a bad thing," says Bari Bren-

ner, a 44-year-old Castro Valley resident who describes herself as "a third-generation nag" with a low tolerance for procrastinators. "I get things done. The truth is I'm organized, they're not. I can see the big *picture.* They can't. We're going on a trip to England. 'Did you call the travel agent?' 'No.' 'Well, *call* the travel agent . . . book the hotel . . . call *now!*' It's the same thing at work. Nagging can be a means to an end."

6 Professional Nags—people who do it for a living—have to disguise what they do to get what they want. "I have to nag all the time—but you have to be careful about using the word *nag,*" says Ruth Holton, a lobbyist for Common Cause, the good-government advocacy group. "I have to ask [legislators] for the same thing over and over again, year in, year out. But if they perceive what you're doing as nagging, they'll say, 'I've heard this 100 times before,' and they'll shut down. There's a fine line between artful persistence and being perceived as a nag."

7 Social nags don't see themselves as naggers. The U.S. Surgeon General's office peppers us with health warnings and calls it education. Environmentalists harp on people to recycle and save the rain forest, all in the name of the Greater Good. "One person's nagger is another person trying to save the world," says Arthur Asa Berger, a popular culture critic at San Francisco State University.

8 Then, somewhere beyond the limits of social convention, lies the dangerous world of the good old-fashioned Domestic Nag. Observers of the human condition, from the Roman poets to the purveyors of prime-time TV, have mined domestic nagging's quirkiness for laughs. But behavioral experts say that's where nagging can run amok. At best, domestic nagging is irritating. In Neil Simon's *The Odd Couple,* Felix wanted Oscar to clean up his act. Oscar liked being a slob, Felix nagged, nothing changed, and Felix finally moved out. At its worst, domestic nagging is murderous. In England last May, a 44-year-old businessman strangled his wife after 15 years of her nagging finally made him snap. In January, a judge ruled that the wife's verbal abuse justifiably provoked him and gave the husband an 18-month suspended sentence.

9 What causes this dynamic of domestic demolition? At the root of nagging, behavioralists say, lies a battle for control. It begins with a legitimate request: "I need you to hear me . . . to be with me . . . to be around, to do things like take out the garbage." But the person being asked doesn't want to change

and sees the request as a threat to his or her control of the status quo. So the request is ignored.

10   "From the nagger's point of view, the naggee isn't listening," says Andrew Christensen, a UCLA psychology professor who has studied nagging for four years. "From there, it escalates. The further you withdraw, the more I nag. The naggee's point of view is, 'If I don't respond, maybe you'll shut up.' " The original request gets lost in the power struggle. The nagging takes on a life of its own. The desperate refrain of "Take out the garbage" can stand for a whole universe of complaints, from "You never do anything around here" to "I hate your stupid brown shoes!" "Sometimes I go through the house saying, 'Dammit, close the cupboards! Don't leave the towels on the floor! What's so hard about moving a vacuum cleaner across the hall. . . .' Bang! Bang! Bang! The list goes on," says a 40-year-old Mill Valley mother of two schoolchildren. "It's like the tape is stuck on replay and nobody's listening."

11   UCLA's Christensen calls it the "demand-withdraw pattern." In 60 percent of the couples he's studied, women were in the demanding, or nagging, role. In 30 percent of the cases, men were the demanders. In 10 percent, the roles were equal. "It may be that, traditionally, women have been more interested in closeness and sharing feelings, and men have been more interested in privacy," he says.

12   The scenario of the man coming home from work and the woman spending the day with the kids feeds the gender stereotype of the female nag. "He wants to sit in front of the TV, she's primed to have an empathetic listener," Christensen says. "The reverse is true with sex. There, men tend to be in the nagging role. Either way, one feels abandoned, neglected, and deprived, the other feels intruded upon. It's a stalemate."

13   Communications experts say there is a way to end the nagging. Both people have the power to stop. What it takes is earnest willingness to step out of the ritual. The naggee could say: "You keep bringing up the issue of the garbage. I'd like to sit down and talk about it." But the gesture would have to be heartfelt, not an exercise in lip service. The nagger could write a note instead of carping. "People tend to react differently to written communication," says Zilbergeld. In either case, the effect is paradoxical: When the nagger stops, it leaves room for the naggee to act. When the naggee listens, there's nothing to nag about.

14   And if it doesn't stop? "It gets more and more robotic," says Gahan Wilson, the *New Yorker* magazine artist who explored the fate of the Nag Eternal in a recent cartoon. "We spend much of our lives on automatic pilot."

EXERCISE 1 Vocabulary Highlights

Write a short definition of each word as it is used in the reading selection. (Paragraph numbers are given in parentheses.) Be prepared to use the words in your own sentences.

crescendoing (1)
timbre (1)
advocacy (adj.) (6)
purveyors (8)
demolition (9)

status quo (9)
escalates (10)
scenario (12)
stalemate (12)
paradoxical (13)

EXERCISE 2 Discussion and Critical Thinking

1. What is being classified?

2. What is the classification based on?

3. Where is the thesis stated?

4. Translate the basic parts of the classification into a simple topic outline.

   I. _____   III. _____
      A. _____   A. _____
      B. _____   B. _____
   II. _____   IV. _____
      A. _____   A. _____
      B. _____   B. _____

Copyright © Houghton Mifflin Company. All rights reserved.

5. What do the behavioralists say is at the root of nagging?

6. How does the idea of control relate to each of the four groups of naggers?

7. How do you react to nagging from family and close friends?

8. Do some people like to be nagged and even depend on naggers for direction?

How to Deal with a Difficult Boss
Donna Brown Hogarty

> *Journalist Donna Brown Hogarty makes it clear that if you've ever had a boss, you've had a bad boss in certain respects. Bosses who are particularly bad, she says, can be grouped in five categories, and being able to recognize the kind of bad boss you have is the first step in dealing with discomfort and frustration at work. This article was published in* Reader's Digest *in 1993.*

1   Harvey Gittler knew his new boss was high-strung—the two had worked together on the factory floor. But Gittler was not prepared for his coworker's personality change when the man was promoted to plant manager.

2   Just two days later, the boss angrily ordered a standing desk removed because he'd seen a worker leaning on it to look up an order. He routinely dressed down employees at the top of his lungs. At one time or another he threatened to fire almost everyone in the plant. And after employees went home, he searched through trash cans for evidence of treason.

3   For many workers, Gittler's experience is frighteningly familiar. Millions of Americans have temperamental bosses. In a 1984 Center for Creative Leadership study of corporate executives, nearly 75 percent of the subjects reported having had at least one intolerable boss.

4   "Virtually all bosses are problem bosses, in one way or another," says psychologist Mardy Grothe, co-author with Peter Wylie of *Problem Bosses: Who They Are and How to Deal with Them.* The reason, he said, lies in lack of training. Most bosses were promoted to management because they excelled at earlier jobs—not because they have experience motivating others.

5   Uncertain economic times worsen the bad-boss syndrome. "There is an acceptance of getting results at any price," says Stanley Bing, a business executive and author of *Crazy Bosses*. "As a result, the people corporations select to be bosses are the most rigid and demanding, and the least able to roll with the punches."

6   Bad bosses often have a recognizable *modus operandi*. Harry Levinson, a management psychologist in Waltham, Massachusetts, has catalogued problem bosses, from the bully to the jellyfish to the disapproving perfectionist. If you're suffering from a bad boss, chances are he or she combines several of these traits and can be dealt with effectively if you use the right strategy.

The Bully

7   During his first week on the job, a new account manager at a small Pennsylvania advertising agency agreed to return some materials to a client. When he mentioned this at a staff meeting, the boss turned beet red, his lips began to quiver and he shouted that the new employee should call his client and confess he didn't know anything about the advertising business, and would *not* be returning the materials.

8   Over the next few months, as the account manager watched coworkers cower under the boss's browbeating, he realized that the tyrant fed on fear. Employees who tried hardest to avoid his ire were most likely to catch it. "He was like a schoolyard bully," the manager recalls, "and I've known since childhood that, when confronted, most bullies back down."

9   Armed with new-found confidence and growing knowledge of the ad business, he matched his boss's behavior. "If he raised his voice, I'd raise mine," the manager recalls. True to type, the boss started to treat him with grudging respect. Eventually, the young man moved up the ranks and was rarely subjected to his boss's outbursts.

10 Although standing up to the bully often works, it *could* make matters worse. Mardy Grothe recommends a different strategy: reasoning with him after he's calmed down. "Some bosses have had a problem with temper control all their lives, and are not pleased with this aspect of their personality," he explains. Want a litmus test? If the boss attempts to compensate for his outburst by overreacting and trying to "make nice" the next day, says Grothe, he or she feels guilty about yesterday's bad behavior.

11 Grothe suggests explaining to your boss how his temper affects you. For instance, you might say, "I know you're trying to improve my performance, but yelling makes me less productive because it upsets me."

12 Whatever strategy you choose, deal with the bully as soon as possible, because "once a dominant/subservient relationship is established, it becomes difficult to loosen," warns industrial psychologist James Fisher. Fisher also suggests confronting your boss behind closed doors whenever possible, to avoid being disrespectful. If your boss continues to be overbearing, try these strategies from psychologist Leonard Felder, author of *Does Someone at Work Treat You Badly?*

13 ▪ To keep your composure while the boss is screaming, repeat a calming phrase to yourself, such as "Ignore the anger. It isn't yours."

14 ▪ Focus on a humorous aspect of your boss's appearance. If she's got a double chin, watch her flesh shake while she's yammering. "By realizing that even the most intimidating people are vulnerable, you can more easily relax," explains Felder.

15 ▪ Wait for your boss to take a breath, then try this comeback line: "I want to hear what you're saying. You've got to slow down."

16 Finally, never relax with an abusive boss, no matter how charming he or she can be, says Stanley Bing. "The bully will worm his or her way into your heart as a way of positioning your face under his foot."

The Workaholic

17 "Some bosses don't know the difference between work, and play," says Nancy Ahlrichs, vice president of client services at the Indianapolis office of Right Associates, an international outplacement firm. "If you want to reach them at night or on a Saturday, just call the office." Worse, such a boss invades your every waking hour, making it all but impossible to separate your own home life from the office.

18 Ahlrichs advises setting limits on your availability. Make sure the boss knows you can be reached in crisis, but as a matter of practice go home at a set time. If he responds angrily, reassure him that you will tackle any project first thing in the morning. Get him to set the priorities, so you can decide which tasks can wait.

19 If you have good rapport with the boss, says Mardy Grothe, consider discussing the problem openly. Your goal is to convince him that just as he needs to meet deadlines, you have personal responsibilities that are equally important.

The Jellyfish

20 "My boss hires people with the assumption that we all know our jobs," says a woman who works for a small firm in New England. "Unfortunately, he hates conflict. If someone makes a mistake, we have to tiptoe around instead of moving to correct it, so we don't hurt anyone's feelings."

21 Her boss is a jellyfish. He has refused to establish even a basic pecking order in his office. As a result, a secretary sat on important correspondence for over a month, risking a client's tax write-offs. Because no one supervises the firm's support staff, the secretary never received a reprimand, and nobody was able to prevent such mishaps from recurring. The jellyfish simply can't take charge because he's afraid of creating conflicts.

22 So "*you* must take charge," suggests Lee Colby, a Minneapolis-based management consultant. "Tell the jellyfish: 'This is what I think I ought to be doing. What do you think?' You are taking the first step, without stepping on your boss's toes."

23 Building an indecisive supervisor's confidence is another good strategy. For example, if you can supply hard facts and figures, you can then use them to justify any course you recom-

mend—and gently ease the jellyfish into taking a firmer position.

The Perfectionist

24 When Nancy Ahlrichs was fresh out of college, she landed her first full-time job, supervising the advertising design and layout of a small-town newspaper. On deadline day, the paper's irritable general manager would suddenly appear over her shoulder, inspecting her work for errors. Then he'd ask a barrage of questions, ending with the one Ahlrichs dreaded most: "Are you sure you'll make deadline?"

25 "I never missed a single deadline," Ahlrichs says, "yet every week he'd ask that same question. I felt belittled by his lack of confidence in me."

26 Ironically, the general manager was lowering the staff's productivity. To paraphrase Voltaire, the perfect is the enemy of the good. According to psychiatrist Allan Mallinger, co-author with Jeannette DeWyze of *Too Perfect: When Being in Control Gets Out of Control*, "The perfectionist's overconcern for thoroughness slows down everyone's work. When everything has to be done perfectly, tasks loom larger." The nit-picking boss who is behind schedule becomes even more difficult, making subordinates ever more miserable.

27 "Remember," says Leonard Felder, "the perfectionist *needs* to find something to worry about." To improve your lot with a perfectionist boss, get her to focus on the big picture. If she demands that you redo a task you've just completed, mention your other assignments, and ask her to prioritize. Often, a boss will let the work you've completed stand—especially when she realizes another project may be put on hold. If your boss is nervous about a particular project, offer regular reports. By keeping the perfectionist posted, you might circumvent constant supervision.

28 Finally, protect yourself emotionally. "You can't depend on the perfectionist for encouragement," says Mallinger. "You owe it to yourself to get a second opinion of your work by asking others."

The Aloof Boss

29 When Gene Bergoffen, now CEO of the National Private Truck Council, worked for another trade association and asked

to be included in the decision-making process, his boss was brusque and inattentive. The boss made decisions alone, and very quickly. "We used to call him 'Ready, Fire, Aim,'" says Bergoffen.

30   Many workers feel frozen out by their boss in subtle ways. Perhaps he doesn't invite them to key meetings or he might never be available to discuss projects. "At the core of every good boss is the ability to communicate expectations clearly," says Gerard Roche, chairman of Heidrick & Struggles, an executive search firm. "Employees should never have to wonder what's on a boss's mind."

31   If your boss fails to give you direction, Roche says, "the worst thing you can do is nothing. Determine the best course of action, then say to your boss: 'Unless I hear otherwise, here's what I'm going to do.'"

32   Other strategies: When your boss does not invite you to meetings or include you in decision making, speak up. "Tell her you have information that might prove to be valuable," suggests Lee Colby. If that approach doesn't work, find an intermediary who respects your work and can persuade the boss to listen to your views.

33   To understand your boss's inability to communicate, it's vital to examine his work style. "Some like hard data, logically arranged in writing," says Colby. "Others prefer face-to-face meetings. Find out what makes your boss tick—and speak in his or her language."

34   Understanding your boss can make your job more bearable in a number of ways. For instance, try offering the boss two solutions to a problem—one that will make him happy, and one that will help you to reach your goals. Even the most difficult boss will usually allow you to solve problems in your own way—as long as he's convinced of your loyalty to him.

35   No matter which type of bad boss you have, think twice before going over his head. Try forming a committee with your colleagues and approaching the boss all together. The difficult boss is usually unaware of the problem and often is eager to make amends.

36   Before embarking on any course of action, engage in some self-analysis. Chances are, no matter how difficult your job is, you are also contributing to the conflict. "Talk to people who

know you both, and get some honest feedback," suggests Mardy Grothe. "If you can fix the ways in which you're contributing to the problem, you'll be more likely to get your boss to change."

37   Even if you can't, there's a silver lining: the worst bosses often have the most to teach you. Bullies, for example, are frequently masters at reaching difficult goals. Perfectionists can often prod you into exceeding your own expectations.

38   As a young resident psychologist at the Menninger psychiatric hospital in Topeka, Kansas, Harry Levinson was initially overwhelmed by the high standards of founder Karl Menninger. "I felt I was never going to be able to diagnose patients as well as he did or perform to such high academic requirements," Levinson recalls. He even considered quitting. But in the end, he rose to the challenge, and today he believes he owes much of his success to what he learned during that critical period.

39   Dealing with a difficult boss forces you to set priorities, to overcome fears, to stay calm under the gun, and to negotiate for better working conditions. And the skills you sharpen to ease a tense relationship will stand you in good stead throughout your career. "Employees who are able to survive a trying boss often earn the respect of higher-ups for their ability to manage a situation," says Levinson. "And because a difficult boss can cause rapid turnover, those who stick it out often advance quickly."

40   Your bad boss can also teach you what *not* to do with subordinates as you move up—and one day enable you to be a better boss yourself.

EXERCISE 3   Vocabulary Highlights

Write a short definition of each word as it is used in the reading selection. (Paragraph numbers are given in parentheses.) Be prepared to use the words in your own sentences.

modus operandi (6)
cower (8)
browbeating (8)
litmus test (10)
subservient (12)
vulnerable (14)

invades (17)
rapport (19)
recurring (21)
paraphrase (26)
prioritize (27)
brusque (29)

EXERCISE 4 Discussion and Critical Thinking

1. What is being classified?

2. What is the purpose of the classification?

3. What are the five classes of bad bosses?

4. Of the five classes, which is the most difficult for most people to deal with? for you to deal with? Can you give any examples?

5. Hogarty suggests that sometimes the boss's behavior is caused to some extent by the behavior of the workers. How would you explain that? Provide examples, if possible.

6. Which of the five types of behavior are sometimes found in combination?

EXERCISE 5 Connecting the Paired Sources

For quick reference, these are the classes discussed in the essays:

Naggers (Hogan): friendly, professional, social, domestic

Bad bosses (Hogarty): bully, workaholic, perfectionist, jellyfish, aloof boss

1. Assuming that domestic nags can be like bosses and can vary in the same way, to what classes of bad bosses might the domestic nags be similar?

2. Would you deal with the extremely aggressive domestic nagger and the bully bad boss in the same way? Note that in Hogarty's essay, one person suggested confrontation, even yelling back, and another advised against that tactic. What factors are different in the two situations?

3. Of the five groups in the Hogarty essay, which ones are most inclined to be naggers?

4. Which of Hogarty's groups are likely to be especially concerned with control? Rank them from most concerned to least concerned.

5. In regard to control, is the main difference between naggers and bad bosses one of causes or one of effects?

Topics for Using Classification in Writing
Reading-Related Topics
"Why We Carp and Harp"
1. Pick one of the classes of naggers (such as domestic) and show in a paragraph or essay how the category can be divided into subclasses.

2. Write a paper in which you classify people who are frequently nagged (the naggees), such as those in a family, at work, and at school.
3. Using Hogan's set of classes as a framework, discuss each kind of nagger with examples from your experience and your reading.
4. In a paragraph or essay, discuss how the idea of control can be related to each of Hogan's four classes.

"How to Deal with a Difficult Boss"

5. Write about three or more types of bad bosses, giving examples from your own experience.
6. Discuss a subdivision of the bully bosses (such as those who use words, threats of job loss, and physical threats) and explain how each functions.
7. Discuss how the idea of control can be related to the five classes of bad bosses. For example, does the perfectionist seek perfection or merely control?
8. Using this article as a framework, write a classification of good bosses.
9. Hogarty mentions that bad bosses are often made worse by bad employees. Write a classification of bad employees, perhaps from a good boss's perspective.

Paired Sources on Ways of Controlling

10. Discuss the extent to which the four types of naggers are like bosses (either good or bad).
11. Discuss whether the idea of control is good or bad, necessary or unnecessary in nagging and bossing. Is the desire to control always bad? Use the authors' patterns of classification as a framework.
12. Use the same idea as in question 11, but use only one essay as a framework.

Career-Related Topics

13. Discuss the different types of managers you have encountered (democratic, authoritative, autocratic, buddy, aloof).
14. Discuss the different types of customers with whom you have dealt (perhaps according to their purpose for seeking your services or products).

15. Discuss the different types of employees you have observed.
16. Discuss the different qualities of products or services in a particular field.
17. Discuss the different kinds of chat rooms on the Internet.

General Topics

Write a paragraph or an essay using one of the topics listed here. Divide your topic into groups according to a single principle.

18. Intelligence
19. Waitresses
20. Dates
21. Smokers
22. Smiles
23. Liars
24. Gossips
25. TV watchers
26. Clothing styles
27. Sports
28. Dopers
29. Sports fans
30. Churchgoers
31. Laughs
32. Bus drivers
33. Bus or airplane passengers
34. Junk food
35. Graffiti
36. Home computers
37. Mothers or fathers
38. Rock music
39. Telephone talkers
40. Pick-up lines (as in a bar)
41. Chicken eaters
42. Surfers (Internet or ocean)
43. Beards
44. Pet owners

7

Process Analysis: Writing About Doing

At a Glance: Using Process Analysis in Writing

1. Decide whether your process analysis is mainly directive (how to do something) or informative (how you did something or how something occurred). Be appropriately consistent in using pronouns and other designations.

   - For the directive analysis, use the second person, addressing the reader as *you*. The *you* may be understood, even if it is not written.
   - For the informative analysis, use the first person, speaking as *I* or *we*, or the third person, speaking about the subject as *he, she, it,* or *they,* or by name.

2. Consider using these basic forms.

   Directive
   I. Preparation
      A.
      B.
   II. Steps
      A.
      B.
      C.

   EXAMPLE:
   How to Prepare Spring Rolls
   I. Preparation
      A. Suitable cooking area
      B. Utensils, equipment
      C. Spring roll wrappers
      D. Vegetables, sauce
   II. Steps
      A. Season vegetables
      B. Wrap vegetables
      C. Fold wrappers
      D. Deep-fry rolls
      E. Serve rolls with sauce

Informative
I. Background
  A.
  B.
II. Sequence
  A.
  B.
  C.

EXAMPLE:
How Coal Is Formed
I. Background or context
  A. Accumulation of land plants
  B. Bacterial action
  C. Muck formation
II. Sequence
  A. Lignite from pressure
  B. Bituminous from deep burial and heat
  C. Anthracite from metamorphic conditions

3. Listing is a useful prewriting activity for this form. Begin with the Roman numeral headings indicated in item 2.
4. The order of a process analysis will usually be chronological (time based) in some sense. Certain transitional words are commonly used to promote coherence: *first, second, third, then, soon, now, next, finally, at last, therefore,* and *consequently.*

PAIRED SOURCES ON MCWORKERS

At any time more than one-half million youngsters are working at McDonald's. For some it's their first job, an introduction to the working world. These young workers soon get a look at a well-organized industry, one that expects workers to do more or less the same thing whether the location is Hoboken or Hong Kong. Here we have two views. "McDonald's—We Do It All for You" offers insights from a disgruntled former company griddleman. "McDonald's Crew Member" gives a wide-ranging positive appraisal by a current worker.

McDonald's—We Do It All for You

Barbara Garson

In this essay from The Electronic Sweatshop, *Barbara Garson interviews a former McDonald's griddleman who explains why he quit and will never return. It's an inside look at the workplace that produces that burger the same way every time, no matter where you are. A well-established and highly regarded playwright and journalist, Garson has recently focused her attention on workers in a computerized society of service-oriented jobs.*

1   "They called us the Green Machine," says Jason Pratt, recently retired McDonald's griddleman, "'cause the crew had green uniforms then. And that's what it is, a machine. You don't have to know how to cook, you don't have to know how to think. There's a procedure for everything and you just follow the procedures."

2   "Like?" I asked. I was interviewing Jason in the Pizza Hut across from his old McDonald's.

3   "Like, uh," the wiry teenager searched for a way to describe the all-encompassing procedures. "O.K., we'll start you off on something simple. You're on the ten-in-one grill, ten patties in a pound. Your basic burger. The guy on the bin calls, 'Six hamburgers,' so you lay your six pieces of meat on the grill and set the timer." Before my eyes Jason conjures up the gleaming, mechanized McDonald's kitchen. "Beep-beep, beep-beep, beep-beep. That's the beeper to sear 'em. It goes off in twenty seconds. Sup, sup, sup, sup, sup, sup." He presses each of the six patties down on the sizzling grill with an imaginary silver disk. "Now you turn off the sear beeper, put the buns in the oven, set the oven timer and then the next beeper is to turn the meat. This one goes beep-beep-beep, beep-beep-beep. So you turn your patties and then you drop your re-cons on the meat, t-con, t-con, t-con." Here Jason takes two imaginary handfuls of re-constituted onions out of water and sets them out, two blops at a time, on top of the six patties he's arranged in two neat rows on the grill. "Now the bun oven buzzes [there are more than a half dozen different timers with distinct beeps and buzzes in a McDonald's kitchen]. This one turns itself off when you open the oven door so you just take out your crowns, line 'em up and give 'em each a squirt of mustard and a squirt of ketchup." With mustard in his right hand and ketchup in his left, Jason wields the dispensers like a pair of six-shooters up and down the lines of buns. Each dispenser has two triggers. One fires the premeasured squirt for ten-in-ones—the second is set for quarter-pounders.

4   "Now," says Jason, slowing down, "now you get to put on the pickles. Two if they're regular, three if they're small. That's the creative part. Then the lettuce, then you ask for a cheese count ('cheese on four please'). Finally the last beep goes off and you lay your burger on the crowns."

5   "On the *crown* of the buns?" I ask, unable to visualize. "On top?"

6   "Yeah, you dress 'em upside down. Put 'em in the box upside down too. They flip 'em over when they serve 'em."

7   "Oh, I think I see."

8   "Then scoop up the heels [the bun bottoms] which are on top of the bun warmer, rake the heels with one hand and push the tray out from underneath and they land (plip) one on each burger, right on top of the re-cons, neat and perfect. [The official time allotted by Hamburger Central, the McDonald's headquarters in Oak Brook, Illinois, is ninety seconds to prepare and serve a burger.] It's like I told you. The procedures make the burgers. You don't have to know a thing."

9   McDonald's employs 500,000 teenagers at any one time. Most don't stay long. About 8 million Americans—7 percent of our labor force—have worked at McDonald's and moved on.* Jason is not a typical ex-employee. In fact, Jason is a legend among the teenagers at the three McDonald's outlets in his suburban area. It seems he was so fast at the griddle (or maybe just fast talking) that he'd been taken back three times by two different managers after quitting.

10 But Jason became a real legend in his last stint at McDonald's. He'd been sent out the back door with the garbage, but instead of coming back in he got into a car with two friends and just drove away. That's the part the local teenagers love to tell. "No fight with the manager or anything . . . just drove away and never came back. . . . I don't think they'd give him a job again."

11 "I would never go back to McDonald's," says Jason. "Not even as a manager." Jason is enrolled at the local junior college. "I'd like to run a real restaurant someday, but I'm taking data processing to fall back on." He's had many part-time jobs, the highest-paid at a hospital ($4.00 an hour), but that didn't last, and now dishwashing (at the $3.35 minimum). "Same as McDonald's. But I would never go back there. You're a complete robot."

12 "It seems like you can improvise a little with the onions," I suggested. "They're not premeasured." Indeed, the reconstituted onion shreds grabbed out of a container by the unscientific-looking wet handful struck me as oddly out of character in the McDonald's kitchen.

*These statistics come from John F. Love, *McDonald's Behind the Golden Arches*. Additional background information in this essay comes from Ray Kroc and Robert Anderson, *Grinding It Out*, and Max Boas and Steve Chain, *Big Mac*.

Copyright © Houghton Mifflin Company. All rights reserved.

13   "There's supposed to be twelve onion bits per patty," Jason informed me. "They spot check."
14   "Oh come on."
15   "You think I'm kiddin'. They lift your heels and they say, 'You got too many onions.' It's portion control."
16   "Is there any freedom anywhere in the process?" I asked.
17   "Lettuce. They'll leave you alone as long as it's neat."
18   "So lettuce is freedom; pickles is judgment?"
19   "Yeah but you don't have time to play around with your pickles. They're never gonna say just six pickles except on the disk. [Each store has video disks to train the crew for each of about twenty work stations, like fries, register, lobby, quarter-pounder grill.] What you'll hear in real life is 'twelve and six on a turn-lay.' The first number is your hamburgers, the second is your Big Macs. On a turn-lay means you lay the first twelve, then you put down the second batch after you turn the first. So you got twenty-four burgers on the grill, in shifts. It's what they call a production mode. And remember you also got your fillets, your McNuggets. . . ."
20   "Wait, slow down." By then I was losing track of the patties on our imaginary grill. "I don't understand this turn-lay thing."
21   "Don't worry, you don't have to understand. You follow the beepers, you follow the buzzers, and you turn your meat as fast as you can. It's like I told you, to work at McDonald's you don't need a face, you don't need a brain. You need to have two hands and two legs and move 'em as fast as you can. That's the whole system. I wouldn't go back there again for anything."

EXERCISE 1 Discussion and Critical Thinking

1. Write numbers in the left margin of the essay to indicate the steps in the procedure described in paragraphs 3 through 8.

2. Jason Pratt says, "The procedures make the burgers." Is that bad for the burger customers or bad for the burger makers? Or both? Explain.

3. Is Pratt a typical McDonald's employee? What positive things might be said about the company?

4. How are the procedures followed by McDonald's different from other procedures you have encountered in similar jobs?

5. How do you account for the fact that some people work at McDonald's, even doing grill duty, for a long time? Do they like to work there? Do some people thrive on the repetition? Have some people learned to deal creatively with the repetition?

McDonald's Crew Member

Kysha Lewin

In her own dictated words, Kysha Lewin, sixteen-year-old student, provides an account of experiences working at McDonald's as a first job. It is not a polished essay, but it is clear and direct, offering a mostly positive view from inside the workplace of the company that is the largest employer of young people.

1   I'm sixteen and a half. I go to Red Bank Regional High School in Little Silver, New Jersey. I'm in tenth grade. Last year I decided I needed a job because it's like only my mom, you know? She's trying to take care of the bills, and it's hard for her. So I don't get allowance, and I'm still a child, I want to have fun, to go out, not just sit on the porch crying. So when I turned fifteen, I decided that I wanted to work. I heard that McDonald's would hire you at fifteen and I came and talked to the managers.

2   They asked what kind of things you do—do you communicate with people well? Are you good at talking to them, understanding what they're saying? You know? They asked me do I like kids because they wanted me to do birthday parties for lit-

tle kids. I'm like the hostess sometimes. And I love kids. And I guess they liked me, because they hired me.

3   It was kind of difficult at first. I had to get to know the register, to listen and concentrate on what the person's ordering and then find the buttons on the board—it took me like two days or so to really get to understand it. But everybody was very relaxed, kinda like, "It's just gonna take you some time to get used to it." They were very patient with me, even the customers were patient. And now it's a breeze. I just pick up stuff easily. I'm a good listener, a person that loves to follow directions.

4   The only real thing with this job is you have to make sure you're always busy. Because McDonald's is always busy. Make sure everything is stocked, cleaned—if you don't have a customer to serve, maybe somebody else has a customer, try to help them out, back them up, get the food, you know? Look at the screen on their register and see what food they don't already have. Go get it. Work together.

5   They have a lot of rules, but it's not like rule crazy. They've only had one meeting while I've been here where they was like basically reviewing the rules and roles and stuff. It's really pretty straightforward, like with the balloon situation—we just always have to make sure there's balloons in the lobby 'cause, you know, we want to make the kids happy. And we have to sweep and mop every hour. And we have this thing, it's like a timer and when it goes off, everybody in the place has to go and sanitize their hands. There's like a liquid that you rub on that dries off real quick. You have to make sure you go do that or you get in trouble.

6   The other rules are basically you have to be on time, you have to stock, clean up, help out. They also have a rule for fries. You have to be sixteen to make fries. If you're fifteen you can only stuff 'em, you can't pick 'em up outta the fryer. I think it's a dumb rule—I mean, what are we supposed to do if it gets busy and there's nobody at the fries but you and you're fifteen? Sit and wait? Then the customer gets mad. Dumb rule, but whatever. Now I'm sixteen, so I make fries sometimes. I just started doing that. I don't make sandwiches because you have to be eighteen before you can work on the grill. I wish I worked the grill. It's easier and it's better than working in the front. 'Cause all you do is like make sandwiches and there's always some-

body you can talk to there and you don't have to deal with the customers, which is the hard part.

7   Some of the customers can be friendly, some can just have an attitude, and some try to make you a fool. I've seen it many a time. Like, for instance, I was working the drive-through and the guy said he was missing his fries, right? So I gave him a fry. He came back into McDonald's and told the manager that he was missing his fries. He was trying to just get another fry for free. I went and told the manager. I don't know why they think they can get over like that. These people are crazy. They say the customer is always right, but personally, me, I don't let 'em get away with that. It makes me mad. I mean, it's costing the boss money and if he loses money then we lose money because we lose our hours and I can't have that.

8   I work about twenty hours a week, after school and weekends. When I turned sixteen they wanted me to take more hours but my mom didn't want me to mess up my school. So I just stayed around twenty. With schoolwork, I guess it's a lot. But I got God in my life, I have a lot of faith, I'm not tired. I'm young and have a lot of energy.

9   I make five-fifteen an hour and I give my mother about half of my check because it helps. I mean, I live with my eleven-year-old brother, my four-year-old sister, and my eight-month-old baby sister and we get along real well, but my mother works hard. I see how hard. She used to be so confident, you know? And now she's struggling trying to support us on her own. My father's in Virginia. My parents are divorced but they're like back together—it's like a long-distance relationship. But my mother's the one that's supporting us. She works in a nursing home. It means a lot to her that I'm working and helping out. She's covered up with bills and stuff. I see what she's going through and I want to help her, you know? She gets sick sometimes, real sick, asthma. The church helps out some, but still, it's just her. And sometimes I see her all depressed and crying and stuff over bills and I feel bad. I feel so bad for her. I know she did a lot for me and I want to do the same thing in return.

10   My mother says she feels bad about how much I'm working. I say don't worry about it, you know? The thing is, it's fun. The customers and the managers aren't great—my boss, he has a little attitude. Like he yelled at me one time when I was two

minutes late, after I worked here for a year and I was never late. It was only two minutes. I was really upset. My mom was mad, too. But mostly, it's fun. There's frustration but, you know, you keep yourself motivated, I don't know how. [Laughs] But you do. I mean, it's just like—I know I have to go to work, I have to find some way to go to work, and right now I'm having fun, you know? I'm young. It's my first job. I'm getting to know people and I look forward to coming to McDonald's.

11   I got a lot of friends here. They're real cool to talk to, chill with, go out with. There's turnover—some people aren't used to working and they get lazy or they don't come to work and get fired, or if they don't obey the rules they have to go—but still, the majority of my friends work here. And cute boys come through the drive-through and flirt. Like you catch their eye or whatever and they ask you for your phone number. [Laughs] I don't ever give out my number. I ask them for theirs, and I decide if I want to call them or not. I'm not giving my number 'cause eehhhhh, you know, some people like to play on the phone and some boys are just disgusting. But it's nice sometimes. It makes me happy.

12   I know work won't be fun my whole life. 'Cause work is not always about fun and games. There comes a time when you have to be serious about what you're doing, you know? Like if I woulda got like a business job, it would be totally different, not like McDonald's. McDonald's is fast and crazy.

13   So it won't always be this fun, but I don't want to stay here too long anyway. I want to get out of the fast-food business. I was supposed to get a raise after three months, but I never got it. I told my boss and he never gave it to me. So I keep working, but I have my eye on leaving. I know I can always get a job anywhere. The type of experience I got here, I can always get a job.

14   But I'll always be grateful to McDonald's, you know? The majority of people I know first started here or some other kind of fast-food place before they got to a good job, a better job. I'd like to do something with hair or maybe clothes. Or I want to get a job working in the hospital—in the nursery with the little babies. I love little kids. I can't wait till I get older so I can have kids. I adore my sisters and my brothers, spoil them. So I'd like the hospital. But whatever happens, a year from now, I'm gonna have a better job. I have a lot of confidence in myself. There's nothing I can't do. I'm fine.

EXERCISE 2 Discussion and Critical Thinking

1. The larger process in this source is how to get a job and get along at McDonald's. Within that larger process are several other processes for particular parts of the job. Indicate some simple steps Kysha Lewin performs in doing these tasks:

   - Working the register (paragraph 3)

   - Being a team member (paragraph 6)

   - Following the rules (paragraph 5)

   - Dealing with customers (paragraph 7)

2. What enables her to work well and find personal satisfaction at McDonald's?

3. Is she correct in saying that she learned things at McDonald's that will help her in other jobs? Explain.

> **EXERCISE 3   Paired Sources on McWorkers**

1. What would account for the difference in the views of Jason Pratt and Kysha Lewin? Explain, taking into consideration these possible factors: age, experience, general outlook, abilities, and personality.

2. Which view impresses you more? Why?

TOPICS FOR USING PROCESS ANALYSIS IN WRITING

Reading-Related Topics

"McDonald's—We Do It All for You"

1. Write about procedures that you are using at a job now or that you have used in a previous job. Explain your attitude toward those procedures and the job.
2. If the procedures you worked with at a job were not written down, write them in concise, numbered parts. Imagine that you are describing them for a person new to the job.
3. Using some of the same terminology used by Jason Pratt, write a procedural statement that explains how to eat a McDonald's burger. Refer to the parts of the burger, such as the pickles and mustard, as it is to be consumed. Include sound effects. Time each stage, using buzzers to indicate time allowances. Give the process a title, for example, "Eating a Burger in Ninety Seconds."

"McDonald's Crew Member"

4. Using the same broad topical coverage as Lewin, write about your job, paying attention to how you performed it and what you learned from it.
5. Using a working person you know as a subject, discuss how his or her situation, attitude, and outlook contribute to the success or failure of that person. Choose someone with a job similar to the one held by Lewin.

Paired Sources on McWorkers

6. Imagine that Lewin and Pratt are working together at a McDonald's grill. Lewin is now eighteen years old. As they flip hamburgers, give them spirited conversation about the merits (mentioning steps of the process they are dealing with) of the work they do.

Career-Related Topics

7. Explain how to display, package, sell, or demonstrate a product.
8. Explain how to perform a service or to repair or install a product.
9. Explain the procedure for operating a machine, computer, piece of equipment, or other device.
10. Explain how to manufacture, construct, or cook something.

General Topics

Most of the following topics are directive as they are phrased. However, each can be transformed into a "how-it-was-done" informative topic by personalizing it and explaining stage by stage how you, someone else, or a group did something. For example, you could write either a directive process analysis about how to deal with an obnoxious person or an informative process analysis about how you or someone else dealt with an obnoxious person. Keep in mind that the two types of process analysis are often blended, especially in the personal approach. Many of the following topics will be more interesting to you and your readers if the process is personalized.

Most of the topics require some narrowing to be treated in a paragraph. For example, writing about playing baseball is too broad; writing about how to throw a curve ball may be manageable.

11. How to end a relationship without hurting someone's feelings
12. How to pass a test for a driver's license
13. How to get a job at _____
14. How to eat _____
15. How to perform a magic trick
16. How to repair _____
17. How to assemble _____
18. How to learn about another culture
19. How to approach someone you would like to know better

8

Cause and Effect: Determining Reasons and Outcomes

At a Glance: Using Cause and Effect in Writing

1. Determine whether your topic should mainly inform or mainly persuade, and use the right tone for your purpose and audience.
2. Use listing to brainstorm cause-and-effect ideas. This is an effective form for prewriting.

Causes	Event, Situation, or Trend	Effects
Low self-esteem	Joining a gang	Life of crime
Drugs		Drug addiction
Tradition		Surrogate family relationship
Fear		Protection
Needs surrogate family		Ostracism
Wants protection		Restricted vocational opportunities
Neighborhood status		

3. Decide whether to concentrate on causes, effects, or a combination of causes and effects. Most paragraphs will focus only on causes or only on effects. Many short essays will discuss causes and effects but will use one as the framework for the piece. A typical basic outline might look like this:

Topic sentence of paragraph or thesis of essay
  I. Cause or Effect 1
  II. Cause or Effect 2
  III. Cause or Effect 3

4. Do not conclude that something is an effect merely because it follows something else. For example, a recession after the election of a new leader may or may not be an effect of the election.
5. Lend emphasis to your main concern(s)—causes, effects, or a combination—by repeating key words such as *cause, reason, effect, result, consequence,* and *outcome.*
6. Causes and effects can be primary (main) or secondary (contributing), immediate or remote.
7. The order of causes and effects in your paper may be based on time, space, emphasis, or a combination.

PAIRED SOURCES ON LOVE, MARRIAGE, AND DIVORCE

Unfortunately for individuals and society, the title of this section of paired essays, "Love, Marriage, and Divorce," defines an all-too-common sequence of events. Many of us have grown up thinking about only the first two in that continuum. Surely, love is an almost magical chemistry that is followed by marriage as a natural commitment, with divorce lurking out there somewhere—for others, not ourselves.

In these two selections, the authors, writing from detached, professional viewpoints, examine human behavior in objective terms. Ian Robertson places "Romantic Love, Courtship, and Marriage" in a sociological, historical context. Taking Cupid out of the picture, he explains why the practices of loving, courting, and marrying have developed and why they have been sustained. He points out that in a different culture we might never fall in love and would not expect to do so. Moreover, he says, "A courtship system is essentially a marriage market," and people who become partners almost certainly have characteristics in common such as age, class, and religion. Anne Roiphe is also concerned with how and why people fall in love and marry, but she focuses on psychological reasons, pointing out that our subconscious often leads us to re-create what we experienced as children in a family. Therefore, a marriage may be a satisfying fulfillment or—unless the partners work at changing negative patterns—a failure.

Romantic Love, Courtship, and Marriage
Ian Robertson

> *Romantic love, courtship, and marriage are more than matters of the heart. According to Ian Robertson, they are all perfectly understandable parts of our culture, and they do not exist in the same way outside our culture. In this excerpt from his college textbook,* Sociology, *Robertson explains the causes of our loving, courting, and marrying. He says that, often without thinking about what we are doing, we respond to the needs of both society and ourselves.*

Romantic Love

1   The American family is supposed to be founded on the romantic love of the marital partners. Traces of a more pragmatic attitude persist in the American upper classes, where daughters are expected to marry "well"—that is, to a male who is eligible by reason of family background and earning potential. Most Americans, however, tend to look askance at anyone who marries for money or some other practical reason in which love plays no part.

2   Happily enough, romantic love defies a clinical definition. It is a different kind of love, though, from the love you have for your parents or your dog. It involves physical symptoms, such as pounding heart and sexual desire, and psychological symptoms, such as obsessive focus on one person and a disregard for any resulting social or economic risks. Our culture encourages us to look for this love—to find that "one and only," perhaps even through "love at first sight." The phenomenon of romantic love occurs when two people meet and find one another personally and physically attractive. They become mutually absorbed, start to behave in what may appear to be a flighty, even irrational manner, decide that they are right for one another, and may then enter a marriage whose success is expected to be guaranteed by their enduring passion. Behavior of this kind is portrayed and warmly endorsed throughout American popular culture, by books, magazines, comics, records, popular songs, movies, and TV.

3   Romantic love is a noble idea, and it can certainly help provide a basis for the spouses to "live happily ever after." But since marriage can equally well be founded on much more prac-

tical considerations, why is romantic love of such importance in the modern world? The reason seems to be that it has the following basic functions in maintaining the institution of the nuclear family.

4   1. *Transfer of loyalties.* Romantic love helps the young partners to loosen their bonds with their family of orientation, a step that is essential if a new neolocal nuclear family is to be created. Their total absorption in one another facilitates a transfer of commitment from existing family and kin to a new family of procreation, something that would be unlikely to happen under the extended family system.

5   2. *Emotional support.* Romantic love provides the couple with emotional support in the difficulties that they face in establishing a new life of their own. This love would not be so necessary in an extended family, where the relatives are able to confront problems cooperatively. In an extended family, in fact, romantic love might even be dysfunctional, for it could distract the couple from their wider obligations to other kin.

6   3. *Incentive to marriage.* Romantic love serves as a bait to lure people into marriage. In the extended family system of traditional societies, it is automatically assumed that people will marry, but in the modern world, people have considerable choice over whether they will get married or not. A contract to form a lifelong commitment to another person is not necessarily a very tempting proposition, however: to some, the prospect may look more like a noose than like a bed of roses. Without feelings of romantic love, many people might have no incentive to marry.

7   To most of us, particularly to those who are in love, romantic love seems to be the most natural thing in the world, but sociological analysis shows that it is a purely cultural product, arising in certain societies for specific reasons. In a different time or in a different society, you might never fall in love, nor would you expect to.

Courtship and Marriage

8   A courtship system is essentially a marriage market. (The metaphor of the "market" may seem a little unromantic, but in fact, the participants do attempt to "sell" their assets—physical appearance, personal charms, talents and interests, and career prospects.) In the matter of mate selection, different courtship

systems vary according to how much choice they permit the individual. The United States probably allows more freedom of choice than any other society. A parent who attempts to interfere in the dating habits or marriage plans of a son or daughter is considered meddlesome and is more likely to alienate than persuade the young lover.

9   In this predominantly urban and anonymous society, young people—often with access to automobiles—have an exceptional degree of privacy in their courting. The practice of dating enables them to find out about one another, to improve their own interpersonal skills in the market, to experiment sexually if they so wish, and finally to select a marriage partner.

10   Who marries whom, then? Cupid's arrow, it turns out, does not strike at random. Despite the cultural emphasis on love as something mysterious and irrational, the selection of marital partners is more orderly and predictable than romantics might like to think. In general, the American mate-selection process produces *homogamy*, marriage between partners who share similar social characteristics. Among the characteristics that seem to attract people to one another are the following:

11   1. *Similar age*. Married partners tend to be of roughly the same age. Husbands are usually older than their wives, but this difference in age has been gradually declining throughout the century, from about 4 years in 1900 to 2.4 years today.

12   2. *Social class*. Most people marry within their own social class. The reasons are obvious: we tend to live in class-segregated neighborhoods, to meet mostly people of the same class, and to share class-specific tastes and interests. Interclass marriages are relatively more common, however, among college students. When there are class differences in a marriage, it is most often the wife who marries upward.

13   3. *Religion*. Most marriages are between people sharing the same religious faith, although Protestant interdenominational marriages are fairly common. Many people change their religion to that of their partner before marriage.

14   4. *Education*. Husbands and wives generally have a similar educational level. The college campus is, of course, a marriage market in its own right, and college-educated people are especially likely to marry people who have a similar education achievement.

15   5. *Racial and ethnic background*. Members of racial and ethnic groups are more likely to marry within their own group

than outside it. In particular, interracial marriages are extremely rare. Until the 1960s, several states had laws prohibiting interracial marriages, and such marriages still attract some social disapproval. Interracial marriages between blacks and whites are particularly unusual; in the majority of these cases, the husband is black and the wife white.

16   6. *Propinquity.* Spatial nearness is a common feature of those who marry one another, for the obvious reason that people are likely to have more social interaction and similarities with neighbors, coworkers, or fellow students than with others who are physically more distant.

EXERCISE 1   Discussion and Critical Thinking

1. What is the subject (a situation, circumstance, or trend) at the center of this discussion?

2. Is this piece concerned mainly with causes, effects, or a combination of both?

3. What are the three cultural needs or causes (also called functions) that make romantic love useful in our society?

4. How would you rank the three functions of romantic love in order of importance?

5. On the basis of what assets do individuals attempt to sell themselves on the "marriage market"?

6. Why do people fall in love? What six causes (or "characteristics") does Robertson list?

7. In your estimation, which of the six causes ("characteristics") are the most important?

8. In your estimation, are the assets or the characteristics more important? Should they be?

Why Marriages Fail

Anne Roiphe

As novelist and journalist, Anne Roiphe has been especially concerned with the topic of contemporary relationships. In this essay, first published in Family Weekly, *she concentrates on two phenomena all too frequently linked: marriage and divorce.*

1 These days so many marriages end in divorce that our most sacred vows no longer ring with truth. "Happily ever after" and "Till death do us part" are expressions that seem on the way to becoming obsolete. Why has it become so hard for couples to stay together? What goes wrong? What has happened to us that close to one-half of all marriages are destined for the divorce courts? How could we have created a society in which 42 percent of our children will grow up in single-parent homes? If statistics could only measure loneliness, regret, pain, loss of self-confidence and fear of the future, the numbers would be beyond quantifying.

2   Even though each broken marriage is unique, we can still find the common perils, the common causes for marital despair. Each marriage has crisis points and each marriage tests endurance, the capacity for both intimacy and change. Outside pressures such as job loss, illness, infertility, trouble with a child, care of aging parents and all the other plagues of life hit marriage the way hurricanes blast our shores. Some marriages survive these storms and others don't. Marriages fail, however, not simply because of the outside weather but because the inner climate becomes too hot or too cold, too turbulent or too stupefying.

3   When we look at how we choose our partners and what expectations exist at the tender beginnings of romance, some of the reasons for disaster become quite clear. We all select with unconscious accuracy a mate who will recreate with us the emotional patterns of our first homes. Dr. Carl A. Whitaker, a marital therapist and emeritus professor of psychiatry at the University of Wisconsin, explains, "From early childhood on each of us carried models for marriage, femininity, masculinity, motherhood, fatherhood, and all the other family roles." Each of us falls in love with a mate who has qualities of our parents, who will help us rediscover both the psychological happiness and miseries of our past lives. We may think we have found a man unlike Dad, but then he turns to drink or drugs, or loses his job over and over again or sits silently in front of the TV just the way Dad did. A man may choose a woman who doesn't like kids just like his mother or who gambles away the family savings just like his mother. Or he may choose a slender wife who seems unlike his obese mother but then turns out to have other addictions that destroy their mutual happiness.

4   A man and a woman bring to their marriage bed a blended concoction of conscious and unconscious memories of their parents' lives together. The human way is to compulsively repeat and recreate the patterns of the past. Sigmund Freud so well described the unhappy design that many of us get trapped in: the unmet needs of childhood, the angry feelings left over from frustrations of long ago, the limits of trust and the recurrence of old fears. Once an individual senses this entrapment, there may follow a yearning to escape, and the result could be a broken, splintered marriage.

5   Of course people can overcome the habits and attitudes that developed in childhood. We all have hidden strengths and amazing capacities for growth and creative change. Change, however, requires work—observing your part in a rotten pattern, bringing difficulties out into the open—and work runs counter to the basic myth of marriage: "When I wed this person all my problems will be over. I will have achieved success and I will become the center of life for this other person and this person will be my center, and we will mean everything to each other forever." This myth, which every marriage relies on, is soon exposed. The coming of children, the pulls and tugs of their demands on affection and time, place a considerable strain on that basic myth of meaning everything to each other, of merging together and solving all of life's problems.

6   Concern and tension about money take each partner away from the other. Obligations to demanding parents or still-dependent-upon parents create further strain. Couples today must also deal with all the cultural changes brought on in recent years by the women's movement and the sexual revolution. The altering of roles and the shifting of responsibilities have been extremely trying for many marriages.

7   These and other realities of life erode the visions of marital bliss the way sandstorms eat at rock and the ocean nibbles away at the dunes. Those euphoric, grand feelings that accompany romantic love are really self-delusions, self-hypnotic dreams that enable us to forge a relationship. Real life, failure at work, disappointments, exhaustion, bad smells, bad colds and hard times all puncture the dream and leave us stranded with our mate, with our childhood patterns pushing us this way and that, with our unfulfilled expectations.

8   The struggle to survive in marriage requires adaptability, flexibility, genuine love and kindness and an imagination strong enough to feel what the other is feeling. Many marriages fall apart because either partner cannot imagine what the other wants or cannot communicate what he or she needs or feels. Anger builds until it erupts into a volcanic burst that buries the marriage in ash.

9   It is not hard to see, therefore, how essential communication is for a good marriage. A man and a woman must be able to tell each other how they feel and why they feel the way they do; otherwise they will impose on each other roles and actions that lead to further unhappiness. In some cases, the communication

patterns of childhood—of not talking, of talking too much, of not listening, of distrust and anger, of withdrawal—spill into the marriage and prevent a healthy exchange of thoughts and feelings. The answer is to set up new patterns of communication and intimacy.

10   At the same time, however, we must see each other as individuals. "To achieve a balance between separateness and closeness is one of the major psychological tasks of all human beings at every stage of life," says Dr. Stuart Bartle, a psychiatrist at the New York University Medical Center.

11   If we sense from our mate a need for too much intimacy, we tend to push him or her away, fearing that we may lose our identities in the merging of marriage. One partner may suffocate the other partner in a childlike dependency.

12   A good marriage means growing as a couple but also growing as individuals. This isn't easy. Richard gives up his interest in carpentry because his wife, Helen, is jealous of the time he spends away from her. Karen quits her choir group because her husband dislikes the friends she makes there. Each pair clings to each other and is angry with each other as life closes in on them. This kind of marital balance is easily thrown as one or the other pulls away and divorce follows.

13   Sometimes people pretend that a new partner will solve the old problems. Most often extramarital sex destroys a marriage because it allows an artificial split between the good and the bad—the good is projected on the new partner and the bad is dumped on the head of the old. Dishonesty, hiding and cheating create walls between men and women. Infidelity is just a symptom of trouble. It is a symbolic complaint, a weapon of revenge, as well as an unraveler of closeness. Infidelity is often that proverbial last straw that sinks the camel to the ground.

14   All right—marriage has always been difficult. Why then are we seeing so many divorces at this time? Yes, our modern social fabric is thin, and yes the permissiveness of society has created unrealistic expectations and thrown the family into chaos. But divorce is so common because people today are unwilling to exercise the self-discipline that marriage requires. They expect easy joy, like the entertainment on TV, the thrill of a good party.

15   Marriage takes some kind of sacrifice, not dreadful self-sacrifice of the soul, but some level of compromise. Some of one's fantasies, some of one's legitimate desires have to be given up

for the value of the marriage itself. "While all marital partners feel shackled at times, it is they who really choose to make the marital ties into confining chains or supporting bonds," says Dr. Whitaker. Marriage requires sexual, financial and emotional discipline. A man and a woman cannot follow every impulse, cannot allow themselves to stop growing or changing.

16   Divorce is not an evil act. Sometimes it provides salvation for people who have grown hopelessly apart or were frozen in patterns of pain or mutual unhappiness. Divorce can be, despite its initial devastation, like the first cut of the surgeon's knife, a step toward new health and a good life. On the other hand, if the partners can stay past the breaking up of the romantic myths into the development of real love and intimacy, they have achieved a work as amazing as the greatest cathedrals of the world. Marriages that do not fail but improve, that persist despite imperfections, are not only rare these days but offer a wondrous shelter in which the face of our mutual humanity can safely show itself.

EXERCISE 2   Vocabulary Highlights

Write a short definition of each word as it is used in the reading selection. (Paragraph numbers are given in parentheses.) Be prepared to use the words in your own sentences.

obsolete (1)
perils (2)
turbulent (2)
concoction (4)
erode (7)

projected (13)
symbolic (13)
chaos (14)
myths (16)
persist (16)

EXERCISE 3   Discussion and Critical Thinking

1. What is the subject (a situation, circumstance, or trend) at the center of this discussion?

2. Is this essay concerned more with causes, effects, or a combination?

3. What internal and external factors cause marriage to fail?

4. If it is true we select marriage partners with qualities that will enable us to re-create our childhood experiences, both good and bad, then are those of us who had mostly bad childhood experiences trapped into reproducing those bad patterns?

5. According to Roiphe, what specific realities puncture the dreams of romantic love (paragraph 7)?

6. What are the components of (and thus the causes of) a good marriage?

EXERCISE 4 Connecting the Paired Sources

1. In "Romantic Love, Courtship and Marriage," Ian Robertson says that Cupid's arrow does not strike at random. He goes on to point out six characteristics that are often held in common by marriage partners. What idea does Roiphe, in "Why Marriages Fail," add to those characteristics?

2. The characteristics of mate selection described by Robertson (similar age, social class, religion, education, racial and ethnic background, and propinquity) are largely sociological, whereas Roiphe's interpretation (that is, we tend to select mates who enable us to reproduce our childhood experiences with family) is mainly psychological.

   a. In analyzing marriages, which points (Robertson's or Roiphe's) are easier to identify and document?

   b. In your estimation, which set of characteristics has a greater influence on a marriage?

   c. What is the relationship between the two views? If, for example, a couple do not share all of Robertson's characteristics, does that mean they will develop problems in their marriage and that those problems will be passed on to their children, who will then later seek to duplicate those bad experiences in their own mate selections and marriages?

3. On the topic of romantic love, are the two authors basically in agreement? Which one has a higher regard for romantic love?

4. To what extent can these concepts be applied to same-sex relationships?

Topics for Using Cause and Effect in Writing

Reading-Related Topics

"Romantic Love, Courtship, and Marriage"

1. Write a piece in which you relate all or most of the six "characteristics that seem to attract people to one another" to a marriage or a relationship you are familiar with. Your example may support Robertson's views, or it may show that a marriage can be very good even though the partners do not share several of the six characteristics.
2. Write about a marriage that failed because the partners were too different; that is, they shared few or none of the six characteristics.
3. Write a paragraph or essay in which you argue that the assets that prospective mates try to "sell" each other on (appearance, charm, common interests, career prospects) either are or are not more important than the six characteristics that attract people to each other. Use references to the article as well as your own examples.
4. Write a piece in which you rank the six "characteristics that seem to attract people to one another" and explain the reason for your ranking.
5. Apply the six "characteristics that seem to attract people to one another" to a particular culture other than middle-class American. Which ones fit? Which ones do not? To what degree do some fit?
6. Discuss to what extent the six characteristics apply to same-sex relationships.
7. Robertson says that individuals in the "marriage market" try to sell themselves on the basis of "physical appearance, personal charms, talents and interests, and career prospects." Are those assets more important in mate selection than the six characteristics? Or are the assets merely complementary, just factors that go with the characteristics? Explain your conclusion and evaluate the relationship between assets and characteristics in a long paragraph or an essay.

"Why Marriages Fail"

8. Explain the effects of a divorce on a person you know, either the child of divorced parents or a partner in a divorce. Consider both the immediate and the long-range effects. Don't forget

that Roiphe maintains that divorce is not necessarily a bad idea.

9. Roiphe says that "we all select with unconscious accuracy a mate who will recreate with us the emotional patterns of our first homes." Either agree or disagree with that statement and support your views by discussing the causal factors in a marriage you are familiar with.
10. Discuss an ideal marriage (a particular one, if possible) and explain what made it that way (causes). Consider paragraphs 8–13 for ideas on what Roiphe believes makes a good marriage.
11. Roiphe says, "People can overcome the habits and attitudes that developed in childhood." Write a paragraph or essay in which you show that she is right, or one in which you point out the difficulties in overcoming those habits and attitudes. Use specific examples and stress the causes and/or effects.

Paired Sources on Love, Marriage, and Divorce

12. Write about the extent to which Robertson and Roiphe differ on the idea of romantic love and the role it plays in establishing and maintaining relationships. Explain where Robertson's idea of "courtship" fits, if at all, in Roiphe's scheme. Don't overlook Robertson's "assets" and "characteristics" in relation to Roiphe's "unconscious" choices.
13. Write about the relative significance of the two views. Which author presents the better insights? If you had to rely on only one set of insights, would you choose Robertson's or Roiphe's?
14. Write a piece in which you explain that Robertson and Roiphe together present a complete view of love, marriage, and divorce. Emphasize the causes and effects presented by each author. Consider whether there is any overlapping of the two views.

Career-Related Topics

15. Discuss the effects (benefits) of a particular product or service on the business community, family life, society generally, a specific group (age, income, interest), or an individual.
16. Discuss the needs (thus the cause of development) by individuals, families, or institutions for a particular product or type of product.
17. Discuss the effects of using a certain approach or philosophy in sales, human resources management, or customer service.

General Topics

Select one of these topics as a subject (situation, circumstance, or trend) for your paragraph or essay and then determine whether you will concentrate on causes, effects, or a combination. You can probably write a more interesting, well-developed, and therefore successful paragraph or essay on a topic you can personalize. For example, a discussion about a specific young person who contemplated, attempted, or committed suicide is probably a better topic idea than a general discussion of suicide. If you do not personalize the topic, you will probably have to do some basic research to supply details for development.

18. Attending or completing college
19. Having or getting a job
20. Change in policy or administration
21. Change in coaches, teachers, officeholder(s)
22. Alcoholism
23. Gambling
24. Moving to another country, state, or home
25. Exercise
26. Passing or failing a test or course
27. Popularity of a certain TV program or song
28. Early marriage

9

Comparison and Contrast: Showing Similarities and Differences

At a Glance: Using Comparison and Contrast in Writing

One useful procedure for writing comparison and contrast paragraphs and essays is called the 4 P's: *purpose, points, patterns,* and *presentation.*

1. Purpose: During the exploration of your topic, define your purpose clearly.
   - Decide whether you are writing a work that is primarily comparison, primarily contrast, or balanced.
   - Determine whether your main purpose is to inform or to persuade.

   For example, you might argue that one minivan is better than another.

2. Points
   - Indicate your points of comparison or contrast, perhaps by listing.
   - Eliminate irrelevant points.

   (horsepower and gears)
   (safety)
   style
   price
   comfort
   (cargo space)

3. Pattern

- Select the subject-by-subject or the point-by-point pattern after considering your topic and planned treatment. The point-by-point pattern is usually preferred in essays. Only in long papers is there likely to be a mixture of patterns.
- Compose an outline reflecting the pattern you select.
- Use this basic subject-by-subject pattern:

    I. Nissan Quest
        A. Horsepower and gears
        B. Safety
        C. Cargo space
    II. Dodge Caravan
        A. Horsepower and gears
        B. Safety
        C. Cargo space

- Use this basic point-by-point pattern:

    I. Horsepower and gears
        A. Nissan Quest
        B. Dodge Caravan
    II. Safety
        A. Nissan Quest
        B. Dodge Caravan
    III. Cargo space
        A. Nissan Quest
        B. Dodge Caravan

4. Presentation

- Be sure to give each point more or less equal treatment. Attention to each part of the outline will usually ensure balanced development.
- Use transitional words and phrases to indicate comparison and contrast and to establish coherence.
- Use a carefully stated topic sentence for a paragraph and a clear thesis for an essay. Each developmental paragraph should have a topic sentence broad enough to embrace its content.

Paired Sources on Orderly and Disorderly People

Are you fundamentally orderly or disorderly? We all have tendencies toward one or the other extreme. Some of us are hardcore, to our shame or pride. If we lean toward the disorderly, we may scoff at the opposite, referring to them as "uptight" or "anal retentive." If we are in the orderly camp, we may pity the disorderly for failures in work ethic, analytical power, self-discipline, even personal hygiene.

As we read Suzanne Britt's essay, we are probably first surprised and then charmed by her wit and satirical jibes. She insists that the neat (orderly) people are the bad guys and that the sloppy (disorderly) people are the good guys. Moreover, to her, the distinction is not even close. She says, "Neat people are lazier and meaner than sloppy people." She doesn't use the slang term "neat freaks," but she makes it clear that the neat are twisted, self-centered individuals who "cut a clean swath through the organic as well as the inorganic world."

Joyce Gallagher, author of "The Messy Are in Denial," is one of those people whom she characterizes as the organized. Her group has a preordained mission—to save and sustain the less fortunate, the disorganized, the sloppy. A bemused and grudgingly forgiving participant (after all, the disorganized can't help themselves), she traces the history of the organized and disorganized from a recent yard sale back to cave dwellers, saying that human nature hasn't changed much. The disorganized flounder, often in endearing ways, and the organized come to their rescue because of a genetic imperative.

Neat People vs. Sloppy People
Suzanne Britt

In this essay from her book Show and Tell, *Suzanne Britt discusses two kinds of people, the neat and the sloppy. Wouldn't the world be a better place if we were all a bit neater? If you think so, prepare to argue with Suzanne Britt.*

1   I've finally figured out the difference between neat people and sloppy people. The distinction is, as always, moral. Neat people are lazier and meaner than sloppy people.

2   Sloppy people, you see, are not really sloppy. Their sloppiness is merely the unfortunate consequence of their extreme moral rectitude. Sloppy people carry in their mind's eye a heavenly vision, a precise plan, that is so stupendous, so perfect, it can't be achieved in this world or the next.

3   Sloppy people live in Never-Never Land. Someday is their métier. Someday they are planning to alphabetize all their books and set up home catalogs. Someday they will go through their wardrobes and mark certain items for tentative mending and certain items for passing on to relatives of similar shape and size. Someday sloppy people will make family scrapbooks into which they will put newspaper clippings, postcards, locks of hair, and the dried corsage from their senior prom. Someday they will file everything on the surface of their desk, including the cash receipts from coffee purchases at the snack shop. Someday they will sit down and read all the back issues of *The New Yorker*.

4   For all these noble reasons and more, sloppy people never get neat. They aim too high and wide. They save everything, planning someday to file, order, and straighten out the world. But while these ambitious plans take clearer and clearer shape in their heads, the books spill from the shelves onto the floor, the clothes pile up in the hamper and closet, the family mementos accumulate in every drawer, the surface of the desk is buried under mounds of paper and the unread magazines threaten to reach the ceiling.

5   Sloppy people can't bear to part with anything. They give loving attention to every detail. When sloppy people say they're going to tackle the surface of the desk, they really mean it. Not a paper will go unturned, not a rubber band will go unboxed. Four hours or two weeks into their excavation, the desk looks exactly the same, primarily because the sloppy person is meticulously creating new piles of papers with new headings and scrupulously stopping to read all the old book catalogs before he throws them away. A neat person would just bulldoze the desk.

6   Neat people are bums and clods at heart. They have cavalier attitudes toward possessions, including family heirlooms. Everything is just another dust-catcher to them. If anything collects dust, it's got to go and that's that. Neat people will toy with the idea of throwing the children out of the house just to cut down on the clutter.

7   Neat people don't care about process. They like results. What they want to do is get the whole thing over with so they can sit down and watch the rasslin' on TV. Neat people operate on two unvarying principles: Never handle any item twice, and throw everything away.

8   The only thing messy in a neat person's house is the trash can. The minute something comes to a neat person's hand, he will look at it, try to decide if it has immediate use and, finding none, throw it in the trash.

9   Neat people are especially vicious with mail. They never go through their mail unless they are standing directly over a trash can. If the trash can is beside the mailbox, even better. All ads, catalogs, pleas for charitable contributions, church bulletins and money-saving coupons go straight into the trash can without being opened. All letters from home, postcards from Europe, bills and paychecks are opened, immediately responded to, then dropped in the trash can. Neat people keep their receipts only for tax purposes. That's it. No sentimental salvaging of birthday cards or the last letter a dying relative ever wrote. Into the trash it goes.

10 Neat people place neatness above everything, even economics. They are incredibly wasteful. Neat people throw away several toys every time they walk through the den. I knew a neat person once who threw away a perfectly good dish drainer because it had mold on it. The drainer was too much trouble to wash. And neat people sell their furniture when they move. They will sell a La-Z-Boy recliner while you are reclining in it.

11 Neat people are no good to borrow from. Neat people buy everything in expensive little single portions. They get their flour and sugar in two-pound bags. They wouldn't consider clipping a coupon, saving a leftover, reusing plastic nondairy whipped cream containers or rinsing off tin foil and draping it over the unmoldy dish drainer. You can never borrow a neat person's newspaper to see what's playing at the movies. Neat people have the paper all wadded up and in the trash by 7:05 A.M.

12 Neat people cut a clean swath through the organic as well as the inorganic world. People, animals, and things are all one to them. They are so insensitive. After they've finished with the pantry, the medicine cabinet and the attic, they will throw out the red geranium (too many leaves), sell the dog (too many fleas), and send the children off to boarding school (too many scuff marks on the hardwood floors).

Paired Sources on Orderly and Disorderly People **123**

EXERCISE 1 Vocabulary Highlights

Write a short definition of each word as it is used in the reading selection. (Paragraph numbers are given in parentheses.) Be prepared to use the words in your own sentences.

rectitude (2)	meticulously (5)
stupendous (2)	scrupulously (5)
métier (3)	cavalier (6)
tentative (3)	heirlooms (6)
excavation (5)	swath (12)

EXERCISE 2 Discussion and Critical Thinking

1. Is this essay mainly comparison or contrast?

2. Is Britt trying mainly to inform or persuade?

3. What are the main points for this study?

4. Is the pattern mainly point by point or subject by subject?

5. What is the moral distinction between the neat and the sloppy?

6. Britt says that sloppy people are morally superior to neat people. How does that idea differ from common assumptions?

7. To what extent is Britt serious, and to what extent is she just being humorous?

8. Britt presents two extremes. What qualities would a person in the middle have?

The Messy Are in Denial

Joyce Gallagher

Freelance journalist Joyce Gallagher gives us some insights into why the disorganized often marry the organized. She says it's all part of a design in Nature. Reasoning and her personal experience tell her so.

1 Others may see the disorganized as carefree people wallowing happily in the cluttered chaos of their own making. I see their conduct for what it so obviously is—a crying out for help. If they are so contented, then why are so many of them latching onto and becoming entirely dependent on those of us who are organized? Complaining all the while about being controlled they, nevertheless, behave like mistletoe nailing itself to oaks, fleas colonizing St. Bernards, and funguses invading feet.

2 That tendency is easy to document and understand. Anyone can see why the disorganized (the messy, the sloppy, the disorderly, the Pisces, the idealist, the daydreamer) need the organized (the orderly, the systematic, the tidy, the Virgo, the neat, the realistic, the practical). But that leaves the more complicated question: Why would the organized even tolerate the disorganized? Or to use our figures of speech, why would oaks, St. Bernards, and feet be so submissive? I say the answer to all such

connections can be found in the phrase "balance in nature." Every creature-type occupies a niche or plunges into extinction. One role of those who are neat (while they are enjoying their own practical and artistic triumphs) is to provide a secure directive system so the sloppy can experience their measure of fulfillment. Like a stoical whale with a barnacle, the organized hang in there while the disorganized hang on.

3   Of course, hanging on, or even hanging around, doesn't mean the disorganized are always complete parasites. Far from it. In fact, the disorganized are often writers, artists, musicians, pop philosophers, and lovable flakes. They may even be fun to be around, even get married to—even stay married to, if you can get past their messiness.

4   If you will just listen, the disorganized will explain *ad nauseam* their lives as works in progress. And in a sense their lives are works in progress, not in advanced stages of progress such as revision or editing, but in freewriting, brainstorming, clustering. Without a thesis, they freewrite through the material world, not yet knowing what to keep or discard. They brainstorm through life, jumping from one acquisition to another, clustering their "treasures" in attics, work rooms, garages, and other handy, unprotected spaces. Finally, if not directed by an organized person, they run the risk of inundating themselves with their own junk.

5   Fortunately, when Nature has its way, an organizer comes to the rescue—as a friend, a relative, or, perhaps, an official. In my situation, I'm the organized spouse, sometimes succumbing to my disorganized companion's pathetic romanticism, but more often, saving him from himself.

6   I do what I can. As he busily accumulates, I busily distribute. It's not easy. Toil as I might, I look around and see him effortlessly acquiring, like a tornado sucking in stuff faster than I can throw it away. I especially donate to thrift stores. Hapless children, the disabled of all kinds, and veterans of all wars depend mightily on us organized people to provide merchandise to their benefactors. Unfortunately for the organized, the thrift industry also depends on the disorganized as customers to cart home items such as scratchy records, manual typewriters, vintage clothing, and myriad unspeakable artifacts called "collectibles."

7   And if it's not a thrift store providing a game preserve for the disorganized, it's a yard sale. Organized people conduct yard sales. The disorganized attend them. As slack-jawed, hollow-

eyed hulks, they drive compulsively from one location to another, not knowing what they are looking for. I suppose it's an ancient yearning for the hunt, even when the belly, larder, and garage are full. I've known my significant disorganized other to stake out a promising sale site a full hour before opening time, peering through the windshield of his motorized blind, stalking the forlorn, unwanted inanimate prey. Way back in the distance, I shovel out junk, knowing it is the burden of the neat to offset every shopping binge of the sloppy.

8   Despite my taking credit for rescuing and sustaining my disorganized mate, pride didn't prompt me to write this. In fact, I don't particularly relish my lot as an organized person with a directive mission. My behavior is quite beyond my control. As mentioned previously, it's probably instinctive, genetic. Tens of thousands of evolutionary years have made my opposite and me what we are.

9   My spouse's counterpart was perhaps an ancient daydreaming troglodyte, who decorated sandstone cave walls with drawings of hunts, imagining the glories of bringing down that mammoth with one club whomp. If so, there was a well-groomed organizer in the background, arranging his clubs all in a row and his life generally. If she hadn't done so, he couldn't have contributed to the diverse gene pool into which we now dip.

10   Reason tells me that's what happened to the Neanderthals—there was too much inbreeding among the disorganized. Consider the artists' uniform depictions of these creatures: messy to the max, with grubby fingers and tousled hair, their privates barely concealed by scrappy animal-hide clothing. It's no wonder science has failed to establish kinship between them and the surviving relatively neat- and tidy-looking *homo sapiens.*

EXERCISE 3 Vocabulary Highlights

Write a short definition of each word as it is used in the reading selection. (Paragraph numbers are given in parentheses.) Be prepared to use the words in your own sentences.

stoical (2)
parasites (3)
ad nauseam (4)
inundating (4)
artifacts (6)

inanimate (7)
sustaining (8)
troglodyte (9)
Neanderthals (10)
homo sapiens (10)

EXERCISE 4 Discussion and Critical Thinking

1. Is this essay mainly comparison or contrast?

2. Is Gallagher trying mainly to inform or persuade?

3. What points of contrast are applied to the two types?

4. How much truth do you find amid the humor?

5. Do you agree that disorganized people need organized people?

6. Can one also make the point that organized people need disorganized people?

7. Can the high rate of divorce be partly traced to how organized people and disorganized people do or do not pair up?

EXERCISE 5 Connecting the Paired Sources

1. In comparing the two essays, what subjects are equivalent?

2. Britt says that neat people are lazy and mean. Does Gallagher say anything similar about the disorganized? If Gallagher doesn't go that far, then how far does she go in characterizing the disorganized?

3. Are the differences mainly in the types (neat and messy) being discussed or the interpretation of the two types?

4. Both authors use humor to exaggerate traits. Which author distorts reality more?

5. Which author seems more flexible? Explain.

6. With which side of which comparison do you identify, if at all?

Topics for Using Comparison and Contrast in Writing

Reading-Related Topics

"Neat People vs. Sloppy People"

1. Using ideas and points from this essay, discuss two people you know or have read about to argue that Britt's conclusions are valid.
2. Using ideas and points from this essay, discuss two people you know or have read about to argue that her ideas are not valid.
3. Write a comparative study on people with good table manners and those with bad table manners. Explain the causes and effects of their behavior.
4. Using Britt's essay as a model of exaggerated humor, write a comparative study of one of the following:

   - People who exercise a lot and those who hardly exercise
   - People who diet and those who do not
   - Men with beards and those without
   - Women with extremely long fingernails and those with short fingernails
   - People who dye their hair and those who do not
   - People who take care of their yards and those who do not
   - People who take care of their children (or pets) and those who do not

"The Messy Are in Denial"

5. Using Gallagher's points and insights, discuss two people you know or have read about to argue that her conclusions are valid.
6. Using Gallagher's points and insights, discuss two people you know or have read about to argue that her ideas are not valid.

Paired Sources on Orderly and Disorderly People

7. Compare and contrast Britt's sloppy person with Gallagher's disorganized person.
8. Compare and contrast Britt's neat person with Gallagher's organized person.

Career-Related Topics

9. Compare and contrast two products or services with the purpose of showing that one is better.

10. Compare and contrast two management styles or two working styles.
11. Compare and contrast two career fields in order to argue that one is better for you.
12. Compare and contrast a public school with a business.
13. Compare and contrast an athletic team with a business.

General Topics

Make these topics specific by naming the subjects for your comparison and contrast.

14. Two products, such as automobiles, bicycles, motorcycles, snowmobiles
15. Two types of (or specific) police officers, doctors, teachers, clergy, students, athletes
16. Living at college and living at home
17. A small college and a large college, or a four-year college and a community college
18. Two roommates, neighbors, friends, dates
19. Two movies, television shows, commercials, songs, singers
20. Dating and going steady, living together and being married, a person before and after marriage
21. Shopping malls and neighborhood stores
22. Two department stores, such as Wal-Mart and Kmart

10

Definition: Clarifying Terms

At a Glance: Using Definitions in Writing

Simple Definition

1. No two words have exactly the same meaning.
2. Several forms of simple definitions can be blended into your discussion: basic dictionary definitions, synonyms, direct explanations, indirect explanations, and analytical definitions.
3. For a formal or analytical definition, specify the term, class, and characteristic(s).

   EXAMPLE: <u>Capitalism</u> <u>is an economic system</u> <u>characterized by investment</u>
               term   class
              <u>of money, private ownership, and free enterprise.</u>
                          characteristics

4. Avoid "is where" and "is when" definitions, circular definitions, and the use of words in the definition that are more difficult than the word being defined.

Extended Definition

1. Use clustering to consider how you might use other patterns of development in defining your term. (See next page.)
2. The organization of your extended definition is likely to be one of emphasis, but it may also be one of space or time, depending on the subject material. You may use just one pattern of development for the overall organization.
3. Consider these ways of introducing a definition: with a question, with a statement of what it is not, with a statement of what it

132 Chapter 10 Definition: Clarifying Terms

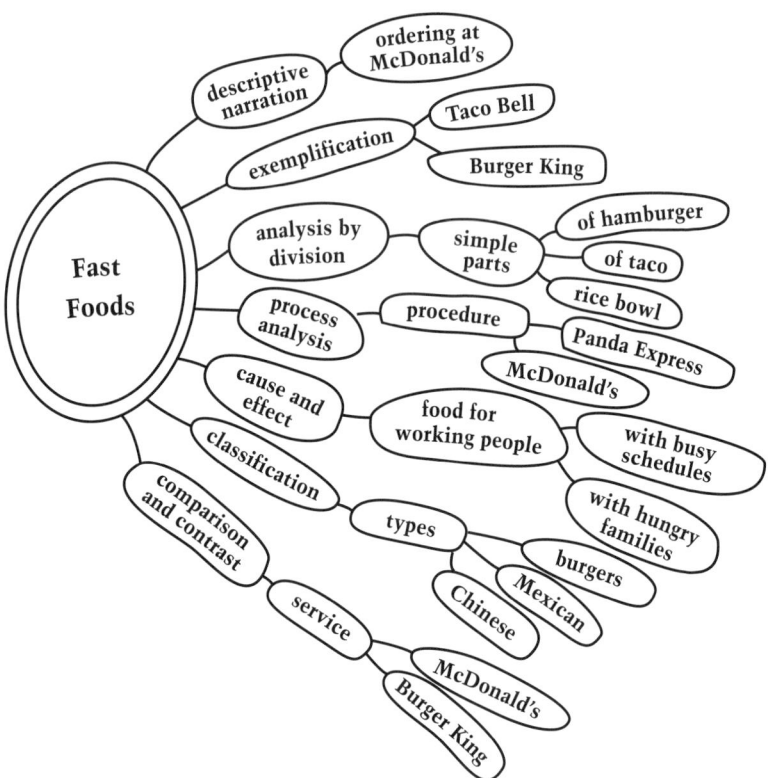

originally meant, or with a discussion of why a clear definition is important. You may use a combination of these ways before you continue with your definition.

4. Whether you personalize a definition depends on your purpose and your audience. Your instructor may ask you to write about a word within the context of your own experience or to write about it from a detached, clinical viewpoint.

PAIRED SOURCES ON SEXUAL HARASSMENT

Discussion of serious issues is often trivialized by accounts of unusual cases. For example, two male kindergarten youngsters were expelled for kissing their female peers, who didn't welcome the advances. Some argued that these incidents were indicative of sexual harassment fanaticism. Others pointed out that sexual harassment is pervasive in our society and that the "boys will be boys" mentality instilled in children is largely responsible for the unwanted sexual behavior—from lewd comments to date rape—of maturity.

Any discussion of sexual harassment is likely to begin with questions. In any relationship, male or female, at what point does ordinary, perhaps playful, behavior end and offensive behavior begin? To what extent is that point defined by the subjective reaction of the offended person? How does one answer a person who says that the plaintiff is too sensitive, to the point of being ridiculous?

The first of these paired selections, "Is It Sexual Harassment?," will introduce you to myths and facts about sexual harassment. The second source, "Sexual Harassment Is No Joke," is a case study for which you can be the judge.

Is It Sexual Harassment?

Ellen Bravo and Ellen Cassedy

From the mailroom to legislative chambers, the debate goes on. It's still not always clear how to define sexual harassment or how to stop it. Here, the authors attempt to show the difference between what's merely annoying and what's illegal. First published in the July 1992 issue of Redbook *magazine, the article is excerpted from Bravo and Cassedy's* The 1995 Guide to Combating Sexual Harassment: Candid Advice from the National Association of Working Women. *The authors credit the consulting firm Jane C. Edmonds and Associates for additional information.*

1   Who decides what constitutes offensive behavior in the workplace? You—the recipient. Try testing your instincts about whether the following scenarios are examples of sexual harassment. Then read the authors' expert analyses.

Is This Abuse?

2   *Scenario 1:* Justine works in a predominantly male department at Company XYZ. She has tried to fit in, and occasionally even laughs at the frequent, off-color sex jokes. But she gets more irritated every day. It's well known in the department that Justine has an out-of-town boyfriend she sees most weekends. It's also known that one of her coworkers, Scott, has the hots for her. Boyfriend or not, he's willing to do almost anything to get a date with Justine. Recently, one of Justine's coworkers overheard their boss talking to Scott in the hallway. "If you get

her into bed," the boss said, "I owe you a dinner. Good luck!" They chuckled and went their separate ways.

3   *Analysis:* The boss is out of line. He probably didn't intend anyone to overhear him—but he shouldn't have been having such a conversation at all. The boss is responsible for keeping the workplace free of harassment and telling employees the consequences of violating the law. Instead, he gave Scott an incentive to make sexual advances toward a coworker. Some may argue that whether Scott and Justine get together socially is a personal matter—but public workplace boasting or dares clearly is not. The law doesn't require Justine to be tough enough to speak up on her own; it says her company must provide an atmosphere free of offensive or hostile behavior. Instead of making Scott think the way to win favor with a supervisor is to pressure a coworker into bed, the boss might arrange for a department-wide seminar on sexual harassment.

4   *Scenario 2:* Freda has been working for Bruce for three years. She has never complained about anything and appears to be happy in her job. Bruce regularly compliments Freda on her outfits; in his opinion, she has a good figure and excellent taste in clothes. Typically, he'll remark, "You sure look good today." Last week, Freda was having a bad day and told Bruce she was "sick and tired of being treated like a sex object." Bruce was stunned at the angry comment. He had always thought they had a good working relationship.

5   *Analysis:* Context and delivery are everything in examining a case like this. When Bruce says, "You sure look good today," does Freda usually answer, "So do you"? Or does Bruce murmur suggestively, "Mmm, you sure look g-o-o-o-o-d," and stare at her chest while she crosses her arms? Does Bruce ever compliment other women? Men? Does he praise Freda's work performance as well?

6   Freda might have been upset earlier about Bruce's comments but failed to speak up because he is her boss. It's not uncommon for someone in her situation to keep quiet for fear of looking foolish or appearing to be a "bad sport." Even if she were just having a bad day, Freda probably wouldn't say she was tired of being treated like a sex object unless she'd felt that way before.

7   Since Bruce was "stunned" that Freda blew up at him, he needs to consider whether she may have sent him signals he ignored. He may be guilty only of not being tuned in. Or perhaps

Freda doesn't really mind the personal praise, but wants more attention paid to her work.

8 Bruce and Freda should sit down and talk. He should listen to what she has to say, then let her know that he values her work *and* her feelings. He should also encourage her to speak up promptly in the future about issues that concern her rather than let them fester.

9 *Scenario 3:* Barbara is a receptionist for a printing company. Surrounding her desk are five ads printed by the company for a beer distributor. The posters feature provocatively posed women holding cans of beer and the slogan, What'll you have? Many times male customers have walked in, looked at the posters, and commented, "I'll have *you,* honey." When Barbara tells her boss she wants the posters removed, he replies that they represent the company's work, and he's proud to display them. He claims no one but Barbara is bothered by the posters, so what's her problem?

10 *Analysis:* The standard here is not how the boss feels but whether a "reasonable woman" might object to being surrounded by such posters, especially since the company has other products it could display. Because women are disproportionately victims of rape and sexual assault, women have a stronger incentive to be concerned with sexual behavior.

11 Barbara did not insist that the company refuse the account or exclude the posters from its portfolio. She merely said she didn't want them displayed around *her* desk. Barbara's view certainly is substantiated by how she's been treated; the posters seem to prompt customers to make suggestive remarks to her.

12 *Scenario 4:* Therese tells Andrew, her subordinate, that she needs him to escort her to a party. She says she's selecting him because he's the most handsome guy on her staff. Andrew says he's busy. Therese responds that she expects people on her staff to be team players.

13 *Analysis:* Therese may have wanted Andrew merely to accompany her to the party, not to have a sexual relationship with her. And Andrew might have been willing to go along if he hadn't been busy. Nevertheless, a reasonable employee may worry about what the boss means by such a request, particularly when it's coupled with remarks about personal appearance.

14 Andrew might not mind that Therese finds him handsome. But most people would object to having their job tied

to their willingness to make a social appearance with the boss outside of work. The implicit threat also makes Therese's request unacceptable. The company should prohibit managers from requiring subordinates to escort them to social engagements.

15 *Scenario 5:* Darlene asks her coworker Dan out on a date. Their romance lasts several months before Darlene ends it. Dan is crushed and wants to keep seeing her. During the workday he frequently buzzes her on the intercom and stops by her desk to chat. Darlene tries to brush him off, with no success. She asks her manager to intervene. The manager says he doesn't get involved in personal matters.

[Analysis omitted. See question 9 under "Discussion and Critical Thinking."]

16 *Scenario 6:* Someone has posted an explicit magazine centerfold in the men's rest room. No women, obviously, ever go in there.

[Analysis omitted. See question 10 under "Discussion and Critical Thinking."]

Exploding the Myths

17 MYTH: Sexual harassment doesn't deserve all this attention. It happens rarely, and it's done by a few dumb—or sick—men.

18 FACT: Studies suggest that at least 50 percent of women experience harassment at some point in their work or academic careers. And though only a small percentage of men are considered "chronic harassers," most who engage in the abuse are not psychopaths. Many other men, intentionally or not, end up condoning or encouraging the harassers even if only by remaining silent.

19 MYTH: Boys will be boys. Sexual harassment is so widespread it's pointless to try to stamp it out.

20 FACT: Yes, sexual harassment is widespread. So is littering. So is stealing. The answer is to stop it, not accept it. To suggest that men aren't capable of controlling their behavior insults men's intelligence. Besides, like other forms of sexual abuse,

harassment is usually a means of exerting power, not expressing passion.

21   MYTH: Most men accused of harassment are just kidding around or trying to flatter.

22   FACT: Chronic harassers *know* their behavior makes women uncomfortable; that's why they do it. Even if women tell them no again and again, this resistance is simply ignored. Other men are genuinely surprised to find that what they intend as innocent teasing isn't perceived that way. In the workplace, a man should assume a female coworker *won't* like sexual comments or gestures until he learns otherwise. And if he is told that he has offended someone, he should apologize at once.

23   MYTH: If women want to be treated as equals on the job, they can't expect special treatment.

24   FACT: A harassment-free workplace doesn't "coddle" women—it simply provides them with the same respectful treatment that men want. Rather than demanding that women adjust to a workplace that's comfortable only for men, management ought to provide an environment that reflects the sensitivities of *all* workers.

25   MYTH: All this talk about harassment will make women hypersensitive, causing them to imagine problems where there are none.

26   FACT: In the short run, defining sexual harassment and providing women with ways to speak up probably *will* lead to an increase in the number of reports filed—most of them regarding real, not imagined, offenses. In the long run, however, public discussion will cut down on unwelcome sexual attention on the job, resulting in fewer harassment complaints and a more productive workplace for everybody.

27   MYTH: You can't blame a guy for looking. Women invite attention by the way they dress.

28   FACT: If a woman's clothes are truly inappropriate for the job, management should tell her so. But a woman's dress *doesn't* give a male employee license to say or do whatever he likes. Once a woman tells him she doesn't like his comments about her clothing, he should back off—or be made to do so.

Copyright © Houghton Mifflin Company. All rights reserved.

Harassment by Any Other Name...

29   Most cases of illegal sexual harassment fall into three categories:

30   1. *Quid pro quo* This is Latin for "something in return for something." In other words, put out or else. A supervisor makes unwelcome sexual advances and either states or implies that the victim *must* submit if she wants to keep her job or receive a raise, promotion, or job assignment. These cases are the most clear-cut. The courts generally hold the employer liable for any such harassment whether he knew about it or not. That's because anyone who holds a supervisory position, with power over terms of employment, is considered to be an "agent" of the employer.

31   2. *Hostile environment* An employee doesn't have to be fired, demoted, or denied a raise or promotion to be sexually harassed and to file a charge. Sexually explicit jokes, pinups, graffiti, vulgar statements, and abusive language and innuendos can poison the victim's work environment. The incidents generally must be shown to be repeated, pervasive, and harmful to the victim's emotional well-being. The employer is considered liable if he knew or should have known of the harassment and did nothing to stop it.

32   3. *Sexual favoritism* In these situations, a supervisor rewards only those employees who submit to his sexual demands. The *other* employees—those who are denied raises or promotions—can claim that they're being penalized by the sexual attention directed at the favored coworkers.

EXERCISE 1   Vocabulary Highlights

Write a short definition of each word as it is used in the reading selection. (Paragraph numbers are given in parentheses.) Be prepared to use the words in your own sentences.

constitutes (1)
incentive (3)
murmur (5)
fester (8)
disproportionately (10)

portfolio (11)
substantiated (11)
chronic (18)
coddle (24)
quid pro quo (30)

EXERCISE 2 Discussion and Critical Thinking

1. Which three paragraphs give a dictionary-like definition of sexual harassment?

2. The definition, divided into three parts, is a good example of the use of what other pattern of development?

3. Besides the three-part definition, what pattern of development is used most extensively in this article?

4. How is cause and effect (as a pattern of development) relevant in this essay?

5. Do the authors go too far in defining sexual harassment?

6. Is having two female authors writing on this subject especially appropriate because the authors can reflect on personal experience? Or does it raise doubts about the objectivity of their observations? Does the authors' gender matter at this time on this topic?

7. What kind of audience do the authors apparently expect?

8. In what way can men benefit from an enforcement of sexual harassment policies?

9. Analyze scenario 5 (paragraph 15).

10. Analyze scenario 6 (paragraph 16).

Sexual Harassment Is No Joke
A. J. Anderson

This case study, based on an actual event, was first published in the "How Do You Manage?" series by A. J. Anderson in Library Journal.

1   The rise of the curtain on this incident discloses the Claims Department of the Charioteer Insurance Company, where the annual Christmas Eve party is taking place. The hour is 4:30 P.M., the day is Thursday, and the sound of the cocktail is heard in the land. For two truant hours the entire staff has been celebrating the arrival of the holiday season.

2   One of the merrymakers is Jason Lowther, an assistant in the Information Center. Lowther is 45 and has worked at Charioteer for 15 years. He is a man who possesses in abundance that indefinite quality known as "personality." A good mixer and storyteller, he usually can be found at most gatherings with

people of both sexes clustered around him like bees on a sunflower.

3   At the present moment he is, as Hemingway once put it, "as drunk as a boiled owl." He is telling a joke—something about a man having had an operation and thinking he has lost all feeling in his nether regions until a female nurse accidentally pinches his "balls" and he realizes all is well. His listeners find it funny to varying degrees, except for Mary Harris-Myers, who is offended by the joke and particularly his use of the word "balls."

4   Harris-Myers also is an assistant in the Information Center, where, along with Lowther and Nancy Richland, she reports to Cecilia Margolius, the newly hired—three weeks—center head. Margolius also has a secretary, Cynthia Eskol. Neither Richland nor Eskol were offended by Lowther's joke; in fact, both found it quite amusing.

5   Now between Lowther and Harris-Myers, who is 28 and has been employed at Charioteer for four years, no great amount of friendship is lost. From the very moment they first met, they bristled with mutual dislike. There is work to be done, however, and both are responsible enough to recognize that; they communicate when they must but keep their icy contacts to an absolute minimum. Richland and Eskol have come to accept what they call this "dumb and bitter feud" as unchangeable and eternal. The former department head did nothing about it.

6   In the short time she has been working there, Margolius has been very much aware of the animosity existing between the two but hitherto has not attempted to deal with it—there have been too many other things to do and learn. It would have to wait until a future date for attention.

7   Or so at least Margolius thought!

8   A quarter to ten on the Monday after the holiday weekend found Margolius working in her office when Harris-Myers appeared at the door. Margolius noticed that her assistant's face was anxious and seamed with deep lines as if by sleeplessness and worry. The tight line of her mouth suggested that something burned hotly inside her.

9   "You're a member of the sexual harassment committee, aren't you?" Harris-Myer stated without any preamble.

10   "Why, yes. I've just been appointed," Margolius replied. "It's my first committee appointment. Why do you ask? Come on in and have a seat."

11   Taking the guest chair, Harris-Myers said, "I want to bring sexual harassment charges against Jason."

12   "Oh," Margolius said questioningly. "Why would you want to do that?"

13   "Did you hear that offensive joke he told at the Christmas party?" Margolius shook her head in the negative. The speaker continued. "Well, I just finished reading the policy manual, and I believe I have grounds for bringing charges against him."

14   "That's a serious charge, Mary," Margolius said, reaching for her copy of the manual. "It can result in dismissal. But let me refresh my memory of the sexual harassment statement. As one of three on the committee who hears complaints and makes recommendations, I certainly should be familiar with it."

15   Two categories of sexual harassment were identified, both of which "have the purpose of creating an intimidating, hostile, or offensive working atmosphere." The first encompasses forcing oneself on another or asking for sex in return for a good evaluation or promotion. The second identifies sexual comments or jokes, violating personal "space," and touching "in a sexually suggestive way." Permissible behavior consists of "normal social interaction; polite compliments; touching that could not reasonably be perceived in a sexual or threatening way; and friendly conversation."

16   When she had finished reading aloud, Margolius said, "What was the joke Jason told? If this goes to the committee, I'd certainly have to know."

17   "*If* this goes?" Harris-Myers questioned. Grudgingly she related the joke. "From what you read, there can be no doubt that Jason violated my personal space by telling a sexual joke. He showed great insensitivity in telling it. I was standing next to Nancy and Cynthia and couldn't help overhearing it. I had no warning he was going to tell it." Quickly she added, "Don't you agree with me as a member of the committee? Don't I have your support?"

18   Margolius's voice was calm and entirely noncommittal as she replied, "It seems to me that anyone accused of sexual harassment has the right to face his or her accuser. Therefore I think that it [is] only proper to invite Jason to join us."

19 Unprepared for this turn of events, Harris-Myers turned pale. "I don't want to be in here with him," she said. "I was hoping you would support me." Her voice shook from the strain of her effort to control it. "If you must speak to him, then please do so without me present." With that she asked if she could leave. The department head nodded.

20 Five minutes later, Jason Lowther was sitting in the guest chair. A bewildered expression crept over his face as Margolius asked if he had told a joke at the Christmas party about a man and an operation and losing feeling and being pinched in the "balls." Lowther scratched at his thatch of greying hair to stimulate recollection of Thursday afternoon. "I was tackling the sour mash bourbon with more earnestness than discretion," he said. "But that sounds like one of my jokes. Why do you ask?"

21 Margolius told him. *Bang* went his first on the desk. "The nerve of her," he said. "She's not exactly Mary Poppins herself, you know. I sit and listen to her use the word—pardon my French—'shit' with Nancy and Cynthia all day long, and she has the unmitigated gall to complain about my word. What a hypocrite! That beats everything," he said, exasperated.

22 Lowther sank back in his seat and stared at his supervisor with eyes that bulged with outrage. His tongue clicked for a moment before he continued. He had to use all his will power to control his voice. "Do you recall that line in *Alice in Wonderland* where Humpty Dumpty says, 'When I use a word it means just what I choose it to mean—neither more nor less'? Well, if I may elaborate: Is it sexual harassment *whenever* the person who thinks they're on the receiving end says it is? What's that going to do to relationships in which men and women are to meet and live and work on an equal plane? How do you distinguish between one person's insensitivity—if that's what I'm guilty of—and another's hypersensitivity? I've told that joke many times in mixed company, and no one has complained before. In fact, I've never been accused of sexual harassment before. Ask anyone here."

23 Having said that he got to his feet and added, "Do you mind if I go for a walk? I could use some fresh air." "Sure, go ahead," Margolius nodded her assent. Her concentration upon her work being dissipated by these disturbing visits, she threw herself on her settee and dropped into a chasm of dark musings.

EXERCISE 3 Vocabulary Highlights

Write a short definition of each word as it is used in the reading selection. (Paragraph numbers are given in parentheses.) Be prepared to use the words in your own sentences.

truant (1)
mutual (5)
animosity (6)
intimidating (15)
discretion (20)

unmitigated (21)
hypocrite (21)
hypersensitivity (22)
dissipated (23)
chasm (23)

EXERCISE 4 Discussion and Critical Thinking

1. Which paragraph contains the definition of sexual harassment?

2. Is the fact that Harris-Myers and Lowther have a personality conflict a factor in assessing the validity of the harassment charge?

3. The incident occurred during what would have been normal working hours, but on this day the staff was allowed to have a Christmas party. Is this occasion covered by the policy manual describing "normal social interaction"?

4. Does Lowther have a countersuit option because of Harris-Myers's use of a four-letter word?

5. Does the fact that Margolius is a member of the sexual harassment committee have any bearing on the way the complaint is made?

6. Is the word used by Lowther an offensive term covered by the sexual harassment policy?

7. Could one argue that his telling the joke is covered by the permissible "friendly conversation" phrase in the sexual harassment code?

8. Margolius has two problems to deal with—a personality conflict and a possible charge of sexual harassment. What should she do about the personality conflict?

9. Many sexual harassment charges do not result in firing, fines, or imprisonment; instead, they result in working with individual situations and educational programs, often at a company level. What should Margolius do about the sexual harassment problem?

EXERCISE 5   Connecting the Paired Sources

1. Which of the three categories offered by Bravo and Cassedy most closely matches the alleged sexual harassment in the case study by Anderson? Explain.

2. Paragraph 25 in "Is It Sexual Harassment?" presents this myth: "All this talk about harassment will make women hypersensitive, causing them to imagine problems where there are none." Does some truth exist in this "myth" as you apply it to the situation of the case study in "Sexual Harassment Is No Joke"?

3. What is the difference between scenario 3 in Bravo and Cassedy and the Anderson case study?

Topics for Using Definition in Writing

Reading-Related Topics

"Is It Sexual Harassment?"

1. Write a paragraph or essay in response to scenario 5 or 6. Use the three categories of illegal sexual harassment in paragraphs 30 through 32 as guiding principles. Be sure your response has a clear definition.
2. Apply one of the three categories of illegal sexual harassment in paragraphs 30 through 32 to a situation with which you are familiar.
3. Discuss one of the myths in terms of its truth or accuracy. Use your own reasoning and experience as support for your views.

"Sexual Harassment Is No Joke"

4. Write your own analysis of the case study involving Harris-Myers and Lowther. Suggest what should be done about the sexual harassment charge. Include a clear definition of sexual harassment.
5. Define personality conflict in the workplace and suggest what the manager, Margolius, should do about the contentious situation between Lowther and Harris-Myers.

Paired Sources on Sexual Harassment

6. Discuss which one of the three categories offered by Bravo and Cassedy could most closely cover the alleged sexual harassment in the case study by Anderson.

7. Write about the difference between the Bravo and Cassedy case study 5 and the Anderson case study.

Career-Related Topics

8. Define one of these terms by using other patterns of development (such as exemplification, cause and effect, narration, comparison and contrast): total quality management, quality control, business ethics, customer satisfaction, cost effectiveness, Internet, temporary worker, union, outsource, downsize.
9. Define a good boss, employee, workplace, employer, or job. Be specific.

General Topics

The following topics are appropriate for extended development of definitions; most of them will also serve well for writing simple definitions.

10. conservative
11. Asian American
12. bonding
13. sexist
14. cult
15. biker
16. liberal
17. workaholic
18. surfer
19. personal space
20. clotheshorse
21. educated
22. gang
23. freedom
24. body language
25. hero
26. druggie
27. convict
28. teen slang
29. psychopath
30. school spirit
31. feminist
32. Chicano
33. jock
34. Hispanic American
35. African American
36. macho
37. cool
38. Native American
39. jerk

11

Argumentation: Writing to Persuade

At a Glance: Using Argumentation in Writing

1. Ask yourself the following questions. Then consider which parts of the formal argument you should include in your paragraph or essay.

   - *Background:* What is the historical or social context for this controversial issue?
   - *Proposition* (the thesis of the essay): What do I want my audience to believe or do?
   - *Qualification of proposition:* Can I limit my proposition so that those who disagree cannot easily challenge me with exceptions?
   - *Refutation* (taking the opposing view into account, mainly to point out its fundamental weakness): What is the view on the other side, and why is it flawed in reasoning or evidence?
   - *Support:* In addition to sound reasoning, can I use appropriate facts, examples, statistics, and opinions of authorities?

2. The basic pattern of a paragraph or an essay of argument is likely to be in this form:

   Proposition (the thesis of the essay)

   I. Support 1
   II. Support 2
   III. Support 3

Paired Sources on SUVs:  or ?

Few drivers are in neutral about SUVs. In this pair of essays, the authors assume polar positions, gun their verbal motors, and gear up. Emotions derived from their experiences color their presentations. Ellen Goodman drives a Saab, while Dave Shiflett commands a Toyota 4Runner. She is obviously sick and tired of SUV transgressions and is not going to take it anymore. He scoffs about charges and flaunts macho pride. Surely you will take sides.

SUVs: Killer Cars

Ellen Goodman

Wasting no time, syndicated columnist Ellen Goodman identifies her enemy in the title of her piece. To her, sport utility vehicles are the pit bulls of the urban motoring world, and she would sterilize them all. She hates SUVs in more ways than Elizabeth Barrett Browning loved Robert, and longs for the days of fresh air, plentiful fuel, light traffic, and friendly drivers. This essay was first published in the Boston Globe.

1   For my second career, I want to write car ads. Or better yet, I want to live in a car ad.

2   In the real world, you and I creep and beep on some misnomered expressway, but in the commercial fantasy land, drivers cruise along deserted, tree-lined roads.

3   We stall and crawl on city streets, but the man in the Lexus races "in the fast lane"—on an elevated road that curves around skyscrapers. We circle the block, looking for a place to park, but the owner of a Toyota RAV4 pulls up onto the sandy beach. We get stuck in the tunnel, but the Escalade man navigates down empty streets because "there are no roadblocks."

4   The world of the car ads bears about as much resemblance to commuter life as the Marlboro ads bear to the cancer ward.

5   All of this is a prelude to a full-boil rant against the archenemy of commuters everywhere: sport utility vehicles. Yes, those gas-guzzling, parking space–hogging bullies of the highway.

6   These sport utility vehicles are bought primarily by people whose favorite sport is shopping and whose most rugged athletic event is hauling the kids to soccer practice.

7   The sales and the size of the larger SUVs have grown at a speed that reminds me of the defense budget. In the escalating highway arms race, SUVs are sold for self-defense. Against what? Other SUVs.

8   As someone who has spent many a traffic-jammed day in the shadow of a behemoth, I am not surprised that the high and weighty are responsible for some 2,000 additional deaths a year. If a 6,000-pound Suburban hits an 1,800-pound Metro, it's going to be bad for the Metro. For that matter, if the Metro hits the Suburban, it's still going to be bad for the Metro.

9   The problem with SUVs is that you can't see over them, you can't see around them and you have to watch out for them. I am by no means the only driver of a small car who has felt intimidated by the big wheels barreling past me. Their macho reputation prompted even the Automobile Club of Southern California to issue an SUV driver tip: "Avoid a 'road warrior' mentality. Some SUV drivers operate under the false illusion that they can ignore common rules of caution."

10   But the biggest and burliest of the pack aren't just safety hazards; they're environmental hazards. Until now, SUVs have been allowed to legally pollute two or three times as much as automobiles. All over suburbia there are people who conscientiously drive their empty bottles to the suburban recycling center in vehicles that get 15 miles to the gallon. There are parents putting big bucks down for a big car so the kids can be safe while the air they breathe is being polluted.

11   At long last some small controls are being promoted. The EPA has proposed for the first time that SUVs be treated like cars. If the agency, and the administration, has its way, a Suburban won't be allowed to emit more than a Taurus. That's an important beginning, but not the whole story.

12   Consider Ford, for example. The automaker produces relatively clean-burning engines. But this fall it will introduce the humongous Excursion. It's 7 feet tall, 80 inches wide, weighs four tons and gets 10 miles to the gallon in the city. No wonder the Sierra Club calls it "the Ford *Valdez*." This is a nice car for taking the kids to school—if you're afraid you'll run into a tank.

13   Do I sound hostile? Last week a would-be SUV owner complained to the *New York Times*' ethics critic that his friends were treating him as if he were "some kind of a criminal." The ethicist wrote back: "If you're planning to drive that SUV in New York, pack a suitcase into your roomy cargo area, because you're driving straight to hell."

14   I wouldn't go that far, though I have wished that hot trip on at least one SUV whose bumper came to eye level with my windshield. Still, the SUV backlash is growing so strong that today's status symbol may become the first socially unacceptable vehicle since cars lost their fins.

15   It's one thing to have an SUV in the outback and quite another to drive it around town. In the end, the right place for the big guy is in an ad. There, the skies are always clean, the drivers are always relaxed and there's never, ever another car in sight.

EXERCISE 1   Discussion and Critical Thinking

Background, Assertion, Qualification, Refutation, Support—these are the main components in most arguments. Professional writers will usually be less procedural, or mechanical, than student writers in presenting them. Locate and discuss the components that pertain to Goodman's essay.

1. Background: What setting does Goodman give to introduce her argument? How does she attract our attention and direct us to her view?

2. Assertion: Does Goodman clearly state her assertion, or proposition, in one sentence? If not, write a one-sentence version here.

3. Qualification: To what extent does Goodman imply that there might be a place for SUVs?

4. Refutation: What are some fundamental positions held by SUV supporters that Goodman finds without merit?

5. What are her main points of support?

6. What kinds of support does Goodman offer? Indicate the specific kinds below.

- Examples:

- Statistics and detailed information:

- Statements by authorities:

Guzzling, Gorgeous & Grand: SUVs and Those Who Love Them
Dave Shiflett

Freelance writer Dave Shiflett is not the David from David and Goliath legend—in fact, he's closer to Goliath. Like the biblical giant, he thunders across the landscape in an SUV long on horsepower and short on charm. Not one to wallow in victimization, he's proud to be driving a socially unacceptable vehicle. This essay was originally published in the National Review.

1   Readers of Dickens* may occasionally imagine what it might have been like to peer from the guillotine and see Madame Defarge† knitting her Book of Sin. One would expect a look of terrifying certitude and ferocity, and while having one's head severed would constitute a profound setback on many fronts, one would at least be without her. As it happens, the old girl has many descendants in our own time, some of whom are glaring at me.

2   The indictment: Those of us who drive sport utility vehicles are guilty of crimes against fellow drivers, the environment, and world stability. We must be left horseless, if not headless.

3   This is a terrible turn of events. The fact is, we SUV drivers are peaceful, humble people of modest hopes and dreams, who happen to like driving around in large vehicles, often because they accommodate our heaving guts, which often reflect an infatuation with the handiwork of Harland Sanders‡ and August Busch.‡‡ Yet when we see ourselves denounced by our detractors, it is as if an alien race were being described.

4   We readily admit that our Big Rides use a bit more gas than the 48 horsepower vehicles (add 3 hp when sails are raised) favored by those who would save the world from us. We are talking about the difference between the 27 miles per gallon average for regular automobiles and the 20 mpg rating of many SUVs. Because global warming is an article of faith among our critics, we're getting additional blame for melting icecaps, flooded coastlines, and the eventual appearance of palm trees in New York City.

5   We believe these charges are grossly exaggerated, and we also reject the assertion that our beloved tanks are killing machines. Official statistics tell us that around 4 percent of road fatalities are the result of SUV-auto crashes, which is of course terrible, but not all those accidents are our fault. Overall, SUVs are blamed for an additional 2,000 deaths per year, though as journalist Ken Smith has pointed out, that number is entirely speculative and must be taken very lightly.

---

*English author of the novel *A Tale of Two Cities,* about the French Revolution, a triumph of the common people over the aristocrats.
†A character from Dickens's novel.
‡Founder of Kentucky Fried Chicken.
‡‡Developer of a brewery.

Copyright © Houghton Mifflin Company. All rights reserved.

6   Our critics are hardly inclined to do so. Sen. Dianne Feinstein, whose calmly sculptured coiffure cannot conceal what some call her Inner Inquisitor, calls us a subspecies of "energy gluttons" and backs legislation that would force us back into the slightly modified go-carts that pass for "mid-sized sedans." Ms. Geneva Overholser, whose placid first name cannot conceal a slightly hectoring personality, has denounced SUVs as "inexplicably popular extravagances" and "nonsensical, gas-guzzling behemoths." Geneva, who was once ombudsman for the *Washington Post,* even admitted that "I feel like a lunatic about SUVs and I hereby invite you to join me in raving."

7   A line quickly formed, A. J. Nomai said the SUV "fad" is "all the rage among yuppies, suburban families and seemingly testosterone unbalanced males." Columnist Ellen Goodman called SUVs "gas-guzzling, parking-space-hogging bullies of the highway." Bullying, as we have come to know, was the cause of the Columbine massacre, so this is a serious charge. Ms. Goodman also insists "the SUV backlash is growing so strong that today's status symbols may become the first socially unacceptable vehicle since cars lost their fins."

8   This all adds up to what crime specialists call a gang bang, and because we are suburban types who steer clear of that kind of activity, we're in shock. This is especially true when our kids join the fray. We understand, of course, that this kind of protest reflects our peaceful and prosperous times. The Cold War is over, and our youth, having had their molars sealed in infancy, have never even worried about tooth decay. As Bill Clinton (who goes around in very large vehicles) said after taking an egg in the ear, it's good for kids to be mad about something, and this is certainly a safe subject.

9   We can also chuckle over the fact that, for many of our critics, mass transit means taking an Airbus to Nice. We were especially gratified by recent news reports that DNC* chief Terry McAuliffe drives a Cadillac SUV that gets about 10 miles to the gallon, while Dick Gephardt,† currently on the warpath against "energy gluttons," drives a Ford SUV. These leaders, it was further reported, have garaged their Big Rides until the political assault on the president's energy policy is over.

---

*Democratic National Committee.
†A congressional leader of the Democratic Party.

10 Which, it seems, is what much of this criticism is about. We SUVers are mere pawns in a larger war. The people on the other side not only want us all to drive cars whose backseat passengers have to ride with their chins on their knees; they have a thing for windmills, solar panels, boarded-up nuclear-power plants, and kerosene lamps. They also tend to support mandatory-seatbelt laws, antismoking ordinances, and restrictions on home barbecuing. We understand that, in California, they went after weed whackers and leaf blowers—and won.

11 Now it is SUV drivers who are in the crosshairs of the new Defarges, and we're being demonized as irrational and "unbalanced" beings, making it all the easier to whack us. Yet we're not nearly the menaces we're cracked up to be, as perhaps my own story illustrates.

12 My first SUV was a 1989 Ford Bronco II. This was no bully machine, but instead a pathetic vehicle whose first engine went out at 52,000 miles (Ms. Goodman tells us she drives a Saab, which, of course, is just perfect). The Bronco passed into the netherworld after a roll-over accident, which critics will find pleasing. That the 16-year-old driver was doing 45 down a 15-mile-per-hour stretch of Hairpin Alley, swerved into a steep ditch, and overcorrected, may have had something to do with the crash, though one hates to point fingers. In any event, the mangled Bronco was replaced by a Toyota 4Runner, purchased with 138,000 miles on the odometer. The SUV community, as it happens, admires diverse peoples, the Japanese among them, especially since they build machines that last. This one should go 300,000 miles, and because of my relatively light driving schedule that means 20 years of service, by which time we may well have been forced into vehicles that pass muster with environmental activists, such as rickshaws. This is not a complaint. I have sent my wife into training in anticipation of this development, and should it arrive we will go quietly, save for the occasional crack of the accelerator.

13 Meanwhile, our aged 4Runner performs its commonplace duties, such as hauling sound equipment for a variety of humble bands that entertain humble citizens at humble watering holes. It also provides a place to sleep during music festivals and road trips. Ms. Goodman, who no doubt snoozes in her Saab between speaking engagements, should be able to empathize. Indeed, if she would only reach out to SUV owners as she does

to members of other victim classes, she might find we are merely her fellow men.

14 Doubtful. It sometimes seems that another major beef against the Big Ride is curiously sexual in nature. Ms. Goodman makes the point: "I am old enough to remember when the shape of a car was female. Detroit's sex appeal was all curves and cars were pitched to men with blondes draped over their hood. Now we're sold bivouac cars with brawn. It's no accident, one reader reminded me, that the Nissan Pathfinder was nicknamed the 'hardbody.' If the minivan is the soccer mom, the SUV is the muscle man, even when it's driven by a woman."*

15 Taken together with the observation about "testosterone unbalanced males," we start to sense that our critics are not merely out to park vehicles. They believe they're shutting down the four-wheeled version of the stag room. Many of us do not understand how people got such an idea, though we are somewhat comforted in knowing that perhaps we're not the only loons in this dispute.

---

*This Goodman quote is from a second "follow-up" column written in response to readers' reactions to the first.

EXERCISE 2   Vocabulary Highlights

Write a short definition of each word as it is used in the reading selection. (Paragraph numbers are given in parentheses.) Be prepared to use the words in your own sentences.

certitude (1)   behemoths (6)
ferocity (1)   ombudsman (6)
coiffure (6)   nether (12)
placid (6)   empathize (13)
hectoring (6)   bivouac (14)

EXERCISE 3   Discussion and Critical Thinking

Background, Assertion, Qualification, Refutation, Support—these are the main components in most arguments. Professional writers will usually be less procedural than student writers in presenting them. Locate and discuss the components that pertain to Shiflett's essay.

1. Background: What setting does Shiflett give to this essay? How does he attract our attention and move us into his argument?

2. Assertion: Does Shiflett clearly state his assertion, or proposition? If not, write a one-sentence version here.

3. Qualification: To what extent does Shiflett limit his assertion that SUVs are admirable?

4. Refutation: What are some fundamental positions held by critics of SUVs that Shiflett finds without merit?

5. What are his main points of support?

6. What kinds of support does Shiflett offer? Indicate the specific kinds below.

- Examples:

158 Chapter 11 *Argumentation: Writing to Persuade*

- Statistics and detailed information:

- Statements by authorities:

EXERCISE 4 Connecting the Paired Sources

1. Which author do you find more convincing? Why?

2. Shiflett refers directly to Goodman's column. If Goodman had the opportunity to review Shiflett's essay, what do you think she would say?

TOPICS FOR USING ARGUMENTATION IN WRITING
Reading-Related Topics
"SUVs: Killer Cars"

1. Write an essay in which you mainly agree or disagree with Goodman's main points. Refer to your own experiences, as well as to other sources if you have any.
2. Use this essay as a model to write about snowmobiles, jet skis, or off-road vehicles.

"Guzzling, Gorgeous & Grand: SUVs and Those Who Love Them"

3. Write an essay in which you mainly agree or disagree with Shiflett's main points. Refer to your own experiences, as well as to other sources if you have any.
4. Use this essay as a model to write about snowmobiles, jet skis, or off-road vehicles.

Paired Sources on SUVs: 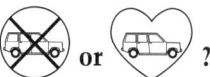 ?

5. Write an essay of argumentation reflecting your own opinion of SUVs. Refer directly to both essays. Include your views and accounts of some of your experiences.

Career-Related Topics

6. Write an essay of argument to convince people that workers at a particular company should or should not be laid off.
7. Write an essay of argument to convince people that workers in a particular service industry should or should not go on strike.

General Topics

The following are broad subject areas; you will have to limit your focus for an essay of argument. You may modify the topics to fit specific situations.

8. Sexual harassment
9. Juvenile justice
10. Endangered species legislation
11. Advertising tobacco
12. Homelessness
13. State-run lotteries
14. Jury reform
15. Legalizing prostitution
16. Censoring rap or rock music
17. Cost of illegal immigration
18. Installation of local traffic signs
19. Foot patrols by local police
20. Change in (your) college registration procedure
21. Local rapid transit
22. Surveillance by video (on campus, in neighborhoods, or in shopping areas)
23. Zone changes for stores selling liquor
24. Curfew for teenagers
25. Laws keeping known gang members out of parks

12

Mixed Patterns

At a Glance: Using Mixed Patterns in Writing

One rarely finds a single pattern in any composition longer than a paragraph. For example, a narrative about a social movement may show cause and effect, define a term, *and* persuade a reader to take action. The advantage of learning to recognize patterns is that although a single pattern can often provide the framework for an assignment, it will almost always be supported by other patterns to some extent.

Unlike the other paired sources in this book, these readings are grouped only thematically. In form, they include four essays, a short story, and a poem. These pairs should be read mainly for subject material. The suggested writing topics will vary by pattern, depending on how the subject material needs to be addressed. One set of topics may include several patterns.

The short story can be read simply as a narrative. Chapter 2 briefly discusses the narrative form (see pages 14–15). Though rich in images and figures of speech (comparisons of unlike things to show common characteristics), the poem "Sympathy" is uncomplicated and can be underlined and annotated for reading techniques just as the other selections.

> **PAIRED SOURCES ON PROGRESS AND PERSPECTIVE**
>
> Change may be the most conspicuous constant of this time, but change does not always denote progress. In this pair of sources, both authors respect the earth, but their views on progress differ.

> Alan Thein Durning celebrates inventions such as the bicycle and ceiling fan as significant human breakthroughs in solving everyday problems. John (Fire) Lame Deer questions all devices and developments that separate human beings from nature, and he seems to believe that most changes have done just that.

The Seven Sustainable Wonders of the World
Alan Thein Durning

Alan Thein Durning is the director of Northwest Environment Watch in Seattle and author of This Place on Earth *(1996). This essay first appeared in the* Utne Reader.

1 I've never seen any of the Seven Wonders of the World, and to tell you the truth I wouldn't really want to. To me, the real wonders are all the little things—little things that work, especially when they do it without hurting the earth. Here's my list of simple things that, though we take them for granted, are absolute wonders. These implements solve every-day problems so elegantly that everyone in the world today—and everyone who is likely to live in it in the next century—could make use of them without Mother Nature's being any the worse for wear.

1. The Bicycle

2 The most thermodynamically efficient transportation device ever created and the most widely used private vehicle in the world, the bicycle lets you travel three times as far on a plateful of calories as you could walking. And they're 53 times more energy efficient—comparing food calories with gasoline calories—than the typical car. Not to mention the fact that they don't pollute the air, lead to oil spills (and oil wars), change the climate, send cities sprawling over the countryside, lock up half of urban space in roads and parking lots, or kill a quarter million people in traffic accidents each year.

3 The world doesn't yet have enough bikes for everybody to ride, but it's getting there quickly: Best estimates put the world's expanding fleet of two-wheelers at 850 million—double the number of autos. We Americans have no excuses on this count: We have more bikes per person than China, where they are the principal vehicle. We just don't ride them much.

2. The Ceiling Fan

4   Appropriate technology's answer to air conditioning, ceiling fans cool tens of millions of people in Asia and Africa. A fan over your bed brings relief in sweltering climes, as I've had plenty of time to reflect on during episodes of digestive turmoil in cheap tropical hotels.

5   Air conditioning, found in two-thirds of U.S. homes, is a juice hog and the bane of the stratospheric ozone layer because of its CFC coolants. Ceiling fans, on the other hand, are simple, durable, and repairable and take little energy to run.

3. The Clothesline

6   A few years ago, I read about an engineering laboratory that claimed it had all but perfected a microwave clothes dryer. The dryer, the story went, would get the moisture out of the wash with one-third the energy of a conventional unit and cause less wear and tear on the fabric.

7   I don't know if they ever got it on the market, but it struck me at the time that if simple wonders had a PR agent, there might have been a news story instead about the perfection of a solar clothes dryer. It takes few materials to manufacture, is safe for kids, requires absolutely no electricity or fuel, and even gets people outdoors where they can talk to their neighbors.

4. The Telephone

8   The greatest innovation in human communications since Gutenberg's printing press, telephone systems are the only entry on my wonders list invented in this century, and—hype of the information age notwithstanding—I'll wager that they never lose ground to other communications technologies. Unlike fax machines, personal computers and computer networks, televisions, VCRs and camcorders, CD-ROMs, and all the other flotsam and jetsam of the information age, telephones are a simple extension of the most time-tested means of human communication: speech.

5. The Public Library

9   Public libraries are the most democratic institutions yet invented. Think of it! Equal access to information for any citizen

who comes inside. A lifetime of learning, all free. Libraries foster community, too, by bringing people of different classes, races, and ages together in that endangered form of human habitat: noncommercial public space.

10   Although conceived without any ecological intention whatsoever, libraries are waste reduction at its best. Each library saves a forestful of trees by making thousands of personal copies of books and periodicals unnecessary. All that paper savings means huge reductions in energy use and water and air pollution, too. In principle, the library concept could be applied to other things—cameras and camcorders, tapes and CDs, cleaning equipment and extra dining chairs—further reducing the number of things our society needs without reducing people's access to them. The town of Takoma Park, Maryland, for example, has a tool library where people can check out a lawn mower, a ratchet set, or a sledgehammer.

6. The Interdepartmental Envelope

11   I don't know what they're really called: those old-fashioned slotted manila envelopes bound with a string and covered with lines for routing papers to one person after another. Whatever they're called, they put modern recycling to shame.

7. The Condom

12   It's a remarkable little device: highly effective, inexpensive, and portable. A few purist Greens might complain about disposability and excess packaging, but these objections are trivial considering the work the condom has to do—battling the scourge of AIDS and stabilizing the human population at a level the earth can comfortably support.

EXERCISE 1 Discussion and Critical Thinking

1. Are these wonders discussed mainly as causes or effects?

2. Briefly indicate the effects of each of Durning's seven wonders:
   - the bicycle

   - the ceiling fan

   - the clothesline

   - the telephone

   - the public library

   - the interdepartmental envelope

   - the condom

3. What statements reveal the author's concern for the environment?

Listening to the Air

John (Fire) Lame Deer and Richard Erdoes

John Lame Deer's message for us is to withdraw from the "conveniences" that have made us "civilized" and "advanced" and contemplate nature and our place in it. He says human beings have set up barriers that have diminished us as people and have altered and destroyed much of our natural world. He wants us to rethink our roles and our responsibilities and to spend more time "listening to the air." His message comes through journalist Richard Erdoes.

1   Let's sit down here, all of us, on the open prairie, where we can't see a highway or a fence. Let's have no blankets to sit on, but feel the ground with our bodies, the earth, the yielding shrubs. Let's have the grass for a mattress, experiencing its sharpness and its softness. Let us become like stones, plants, and trees. Let us be animals, think and feel like animals.

2   Listen to the air. You can hear it, feel it, smell it, taste it. *Woniya waken*—the holy air—which renews all by its breath. *Woniya, woniya waken*—spirit, life, breath, renewal—it means all that. *Woniya*—we sit together, don't touch, but something is there; we feel it between us, as a presence. A good way to start thinking about nature, talk about it. Rather talk to it, talk to the rivers, to the lakes, to the winds as to our relatives.

3   You have made it hard for us to experience nature in the good way by being part of it. Even here we are conscious that somewhere out in those hills there are missile silos and radar stations. White men always pick the few unspoiled, beautiful, awesome spots for the sites of these abominations. You have raped and violated these lands, always saying, "Gimme, gimme, gimme," and never giving anything back. You have taken 200,000 acres of our Pine Ridge reservation and made them into a bombing range. This land is so beautiful and strange that now some of you want to make it into a national park. The only use you have made of this land since you took it from us was to blow it up. You have not only despoiled the earth, the rocks, the minerals, all of which you call "dead" but which are very much alive; you have even changed the animals, which are part of us, part of the Great Spirit, changed them in a horrible way, so no one can recognize them. There is power in a buf-

falo—spiritual, magic power—but there is no power in an Angus, in a Hereford.

4   There is power in an antelope, but not in a goat or in a sheep, which holds still while you butcher it, which will eat your newspaper if you let it. There was a great power in a wolf, even in a coyote. You have made him into a freak—a toy poodle, a Pekingese, a lap dog. You can't do much with a cat, which is like an Indian, unchangeable. So you fix it, alter it, declaw it, even cut its vocal cords so you can experiment on it in a laboratory without being disturbed by its cries.

5   A partridge, a grouse, a quail, a pheasant, you have made them into chickens, creatures that can't fly, that wear a kind of sunglasses so that they won't peck each other's eyes out, "birds" with a "pecking order." There are some farms where they breed chickens for breast meat. Those birds are kept in low cages, forced to be hunched over all the time, which makes the breast muscles very big. Soothing sounds, Muzak, are piped into these chicken hutches. One loud noise and the chickens go haywire, killing themselves by flying against the mesh of their cages. Having to spend all their lives stooped over makes an unnatural, crazy, no-good bird. It also makes unnatural, no-good human beings.

6   That's where you fooled yourselves. You have not only altered, declawed, and malformed your winged and four-legged cousins; you have done it to yourselves. You have changed men into chairmen of boards, into office workers, into time-clock punchers. You have changed women into housewives, truly fearful creatures. I was once invited into the home of such a one.

7   "Watch the ashes, don't smoke, you stain the curtains. Watch the goldfish bowl, don't breathe on the parakeet, don't lean your head against the wallpaper; your hair may be greasy. Don't spill liquor on that table: It has a delicate finish. You should have wiped your boots; the floor was just varnished. Don't, don't, don't . . ." That is crazy. We weren't made to endure this. You live in prisons which you have built for yourselves, calling them "homes," offices, factories. We have a new joke on the reservation: "What is cultural deprivation?" Answer: "Being an upper-middle-class white kid living in a split-level suburban home with a color TV."

8   Sometimes I think that even our pitiful tar-paper shacks are better than your luxury homes. Walking a hundred feet to the

outhouse on a clear wintry night, through mud or snow, that's one small link with nature. Or in the summer, in the back country, leaving the door of the privy open, taking your time, listening to the humming of the insects, the sun warming your bones through the thin planks of wood; you don't even have that pleasure anymore.

9   Americans want to have everything sanitized. No smells! Not even the good, natural man and woman smell. Take away the smell from under the armpits, from your skin. Rub it out, and then spray or dab some nonhuman odor on yourself, stuff you can spend a lot of money on, ten dollars an ounce, so you know this has to smell good. "B.O.," bad breath, "Intimate Female Odor Spray"—I see it all on TV. Soon you'll breed people without body openings.

10   I think white people are so afraid of the world they created that they don't want to see, feel, smell, or hear it. The feeling of rain and snow on your face, being numbed by an icy wind and thawing out before a smoking fire, coming out of a hot sweat bath and plunging into a cold stream, these things make you feel alive, but you don't want them anymore. Living in boxes which shut out the heat of the summer and the chill of winter, living inside a body that no longer has a scent, hearing the noise from the hi-fi instead of listening to the sounds of nature, watching some actor on TV having a make-believe experience when you no longer experience anything for yourself, eating food without taste—that's your way. It's no good.

11   The food you eat, you treat it like your bodies, take out all the nature part, the taste, the smell, the roughness, then put the artificial color, the artificial flavor in. Raw liver, raw kidney— that's what we old-fashioned full-bloods like to get our teeth into. In the old days we used to eat the guts of the buffalo, making a contest of it, two fellows getting hold of a long piece of intestines from opposite ends, starting chewing toward the middle, seeing who can get there first; that's eating. Those buffalo guts, full of half-fermented, half-digested grass and herbs, you didn't need any pills and vitamins when you swallowed those. Use the bitterness of gall for flavoring, not refined salt or sugar. *Wasna*—meat, kidney fat, and berries all pounded together—a lump of that sweet *wasna* kept a man going for a whole day. That was food, that had the power. Not the stuff you give us today: powdered milk, dehydrated eggs, pasteurized butter, chick-

ens that are all drumsticks or all breast; there's no bird left there.

12 You don't want the bird. You don't have the courage to kill honestly—cut off the chicken's head, pluck it and gut it—no, you don't want this anymore. So it all comes in a neat plastic bag, all cut up, ready to eat, with no taste and no guilt. Your mink and seal coats, you don't want to know about the blood and pain which went into making them. Your idea of war—sit in an airplane, way above the clouds, press a button, drop the bombs, and never look below the clouds—that's the odorless, guiltless, sanitized way.

13 When we killed a buffalo, we knew what we were doing. We apologized to his spirit, tried to make him understand why we did it, honoring with a prayer the bones of those who gave their flesh to keep us alive, praying for their return, praying for the life of our brothers, the buffalo nation, as well as for our own people. You wouldn't understand this and that's why we had the Washita Massacre, the Sand Creek Massacre, the dead women and babies at Wounded Knee. That's why we have Song My and My Lai now.

14 To us life, all life, is sacred. The state of South Dakota has pest-control officers. They go up in a plane and shoot coyotes from the air. They keep track of their kills, put them all down in their little books. The stockmen and sheepowners pay them. Coyotes eat mostly rodents, field mice and such. Only once in a while will they go after a stray lamb. They are our natural garbage men cleaning up the rotten and stinking things. They make good pets if you give them a chance. But their living could lose some man a few cents, and so the coyotes are killed from the air. They were here before the sheep, but they are in the way; you can't make a profit out of them. More and more animals are dying out. The animals which the Great Spirit put here, they must go. The man-made animals are allowed to stay—at least until they are shipped out to be butchered. That terrible arrogance of the white man, making himself something more than God, more than nature, saying, "I will let this animal live, because it makes money"; saying, "This animal must go, it brings no income, the space it occupies can be used in a better way. The only good coyote is a dead coyote." They are treating coyotes almost as badly as they used to treat Indians.

EXERCISE 2   Discussion and Critical Thinking

1. How should we begin to start thinking about nature, according to Lame Deer?

2. How have we made it hard to experience nature in the good way, by being part of it?

3. Lame Deer says, "You have not only altered, declawed, and malformed your winged and four-legged cousins; you have done it to yourselves." Explain that statement.

4. In Lame Deer's view, in what ways are Native-American primitive home conditions better than those of urban people?

5. How do Native Americans, according to Lame Deer, regard killing and life?

EXERCISE 3   Connecting the Paired Sources

1. Lame Deer believes that the earth has been sanitized and that the artificial has replaced the natural. To what extent can you reconcile his view with Durning's discussion of each of his "wonders"?

   - the bicycle

- the ceiling fan

- the clothesline

- the telephone

- the public library

- the interdepartmental envelope

- the condom

2. How do you think Durning would respond to Lame Deer's evaluations?

Reading-Related Topics for Writing About Progress and Perspective
"Seven Sustainable Wonders of the World"
1. Using Durning's essay as a model, write about your own three or more "wonders . . . the little things that work . . . especially

without hurting the earth." Be sure to discuss both the immediate and the long-range effects of your selections.
2. Using your own value system, rank and evaluate the seven items Durning selected.
3. Choose one of Durning's "wonders" and discuss its effects more extensively, perhaps relating it to some of your own experiences.

"Listening to the Air"

4. Summarize (see page 7) what Lame Deer said. Be sure to emphasize the main points of his concern.
5. Write a two-part response (see page 8). In the first part, summarize Lame Deer's message. In the second part, evaluate his ideas.
6. Select one of Lame Deer's main ideas and explain how it relates to one of society's problems.
7. Evaluate one or more of Lame Deer's views on food, shelter, hygiene, and nature conservation (hunting, landscape alteration, selective breeding of animals, and animal domestication).
8. Discuss what parts of Lame Deer's message can and should be applied in a practical sense. What parts, though perhaps extreme, make us think critically about how much we have lost in separating ourselves from nature?

Paired Sources on Progress and Perspective

9. Pick three or more of Durning's "wonders" and evaluate them from Lame Deer's perspective. (Some might argue that Lame Deer would not necessarily take issue with all of Durning's ideas.)
10. Write an essay from Durning's perspective in which he argues that he also respects nature and that Lame Deer's views are too extreme, even for Lame Deer's fellow Native Americans.

PAIRED SOURCES ON FREEDOM

A yearning for freedom can take many forms and can occur in many contexts. Paul Laurence Dunbar wrote indirectly of slavery and racial oppression in "Sympathy." He says he knows "why the caged bird sings": It sings for liberation. Kate Chopin also wrote of a person who was oppressed in "The Story of an Hour." The circumstances of the quest for freedom in these two works are vastly different, but the expressions of hunger for independence are remarkably similar in spirit.

Sympathy

Paul Laurence Dunbar

In his poem "Sympathy," Paul Laurence Dunbar writes one of the most haunting lines in American literature: "I know why the caged bird sings." About sixty years after he penned that line, Maya Angelou selected it as the theme and title for a book about her own African-American experience.

I know what the caged bird feels, alas!
When the sun is bright on the upland slopes;
When the wind stirs soft through the springing grass
And the river flows like a stream of glass;
5   When the first bird sings and the first bud opes.
And the faint perfume from its chalice steals—
I know what the caged bird feels!

I know why the caged bird beats his wing
Till its blood is red on the cruel bars;
10   For he must fly back to his perch and cling
When he fain would be on the bough a-swing;
And a pain still throbs in the old, old scars
And they pulse again with a keener sting—
I know why he beats his wing!

15   I know why the caged bird sings, ah me,
When his wing is bruised and his bosom sore—
When he beats his bars and would be free;
It is not a carol of joy or glee,
But a prayer that he sends from his heart's deep core,
20   But a plea, that upward to Heaven he flings—
I know why the caged bird sings!

EXERCISE 4   Discussion and Critical Thinking

1. What does the bird feel as it observes nature?

2. Why does the caged bird beat its wing?

3. Why does the caged bird sing?

4. How do these three points relate to the experiences of an oppressed people, an oppressed person, or specifically a poet who has a universal message but is denied his individuality and artistic freedom?

The Story of an Hour
Kate Chopin

The author of this famous story on love and marriage, Kate Chopin, was left a widow with six children at age thirty-two. Turning to writing seriously, she wrote stories set mainly in the Creole bayou country around New Orleans. Her independent thinking, especially about women's emotions, attracted a firestorm of critical attention to her novel The Awakening, *and two collections of short stories,* Bayou Folk *and* A Night in Acadie, *and established her reputation as a feminist.*

1 Knowing that Mrs. Mallard was afflicted with a heart trouble, great care was taken to break to her as gently as possible the news of her husband's death.

2 It was her sister Josephine who told her, in broken sentences, veiled hints that revealed in half concealing. Her husband's friend Richards was there, too, near her. It was he who had been in the newspaper office when intelligence of the railroad disaster was received, with Brently Mallard's name leading the list of "killed." He had only taken the time to assure himself of its truth by a second telegram, and had hastened to forestall any less careful, less tender friend in bearing the sad message.

3 She did not hear the story as many women have heard the same, with a paralyzed inability to accept its significance. She wept at once, with sudden, wild abandonment, in her sister's arms. When the storm of grief had spent itself she went to her room alone. She would have no one follow her.

4   There stood, facing the open window, a comfortable, roomy armchair. Into this she sank, pressed down by a physical exhaustion that haunted her body and seemed to reach into her soul.

5   She could see in the open square before her house the tops of trees that were all aquiver with the new spring life. The delicious breath of rain was in the air. In the street below a peddler was crying his wares. The notes of a distant song which some one was singing reached her faintly, and countless sparrows were twittering in the eaves.

6   There were patches of blue sky showing here and there through the clouds that had met and piled above the other in the west facing her window.

7   She sat with her head thrown back upon the cushion of the chair quite motionless, except when a sob came up into her throat and shook her, as a child who has cried itself to sleep continues to sob in its dreams.

8   She was young, with a fair, calm face, whose lines bespoke repression and even a certain strength. But now there was a dull stare in her eyes, whose gaze was fixed away off yonder on one of those patches of blue sky. It was not a glance of reflection, but rather indicated a suspension of intelligent thought.

9   There was something coming to her and she was waiting for it, fearfully. What was it? She did not know; it was too subtle and elusive to name. But she felt it, creeping out of the sky, reaching toward her through the sounds, the scents, the color that filled the air.

10 Now her bosom rose and fell tumultuously. She was beginning to recognize this thing that was approaching to possess her, and she was striving to beat it back with her will—as powerless as her two white slender hands would have been.

11 When she abandoned herself a little whispered word escaped her slightly parted lips. She said it over and over under her breath: "Free, free, free!" The vacant stare and the look of terror that had followed it went from her eyes. They stayed keen and bright. Her pulses beat fast, and the coursing blood warmed and relaxed every inch of her body.

12 She did not stop to ask if it were not a monstrous joy that held her. A clear and exalted perception enabled her to dismiss the suggestion as trivial.

13 She knew that she would weep again when she saw the kind, tender hands folded in death; the face that had never

looked save with love upon her, fixed and gray and dead. But she saw beyond that bitter moment a long procession of years to come that would belong to her absolutely. And she opened and spread her arms out to them in welcome.

14   There would be no one to live for during those coming years; she would live for herself. There would be no powerful will bending her in that blind persistence with which men and women believe they have a right to impose a private will upon a fellow-creature. A kind intention or a cruel intention made the act seem no less a crime as she looked upon it in that brief moment of illumination.

15   And yet she had loved him—sometimes. Often she had not. What did it matter! What could love, the unsolved mystery, count for in face of this possession of self-assertion which she suddenly recognized as the strongest impulse of her being!

16   "Free! Body and soul free!" she kept whispering.

17   Josephine was kneeling before the closed door with her lips to the keyhole, imploring for admission. "Louise, open the door! I beg; open the door—you will make yourself ill. What are you doing, Louise? For heaven's sake open the door."

18   "Go away. I am not making myself ill." No; she was drinking in a very elixir of life through that open window.

19   Her fancy was running riot along those days ahead of her. Spring days, and summer days, and all sorts of days that would be her own. She breathed a quick prayer that life might be long. It was only yesterday she had thought with a shudder that life might be long.

20   She arose at length and opened the door to her sister's importunities. There was a feverish triumph in her eyes, and she carried herself unwittingly like a goddess of Victory. She clasped her sister's waist, and together they descended the stairs. Richards stood waiting for them at the bottom.

21   Some one was opening the door with a latchkey. It was Brently Mallard who entered, a little travel-stained, composedly carrying his grip-sack and umbrella. He had been far from the scene of accident, and did not even know there had been one. He stood amazed at Josephine's piercing cry; at Richards's quick motion to screen him from the view of his wife.

22   But Richards was too late.

23   When the doctors came they said she had died of heart disease—of joy that kills.

Copyright © Houghton Mifflin Company. All rights reserved.

EXERCISE 5 Discussion and Critical Thinking

1. What is Mrs. Mallard's first reaction upon hearing of her husband's death?

2. What is her second reaction?

3. Why hasn't she considered freedom before?

4. What does she see in nature?

5. How do the images of springtime, rain, birds singing, blue sky through the clouds correspond with Mrs. Mallard's thoughts about the future?

6. How do you reconcile these statements: "she knew that she would weep again when she saw . . . the face [of her husband] that had never looked save with love upon her" and "There would be no powerful will bending her in that blind persistence with which men and women believe they have a right to impose a private will upon a fellow-creature"?

7. Is this story mainly about women's rights, freedom, or some other subject?

8. Why does Mrs. Mallard die?

EXERCISE 6 Connecting the Paired Sources

1. Explain how the poetic speaker and Mrs. Mallard are seeking freedom.

2. In what ways are the concepts of freedom similar and dissimilar in the two works?

3. Explain how the authors use nature in a similar way.

Reading-Related Topics for Writing About Freedom

"Sympathy"

1. Dunbar wrote "Sympathy" about forty years after the Civil War. In a paragraph or essay, discuss how the poem relates to both the time before (slavery) and the time after (discrimination) the end of that war.
2. In an analysis of the poem (see page 172), discuss how the caged bird feels as it observes nature, why it beats its wings against the cage, and why it sings.

"The Story of an Hour"

3. In an analysis by division (see page 53), discuss this story according to the basic parts of a narrative: situation, conflict, struggle, outcome, meaning.
4. In a brief essay, discuss how Mr. Mallard and Mrs. Mallard would probably define (see pages 131–132) freedom or love.
5. Using Chopin's story as an inspiration, write about someone you know who is involved in an oppressive love relationship in which the oppressor thinks he or she is controlling and directing only to be protective.

Paired Sources on Freedom

6. Compare and contrast (see pages 118–119) the caged bird with Mrs. Mallard. Consider using three or more of these points as they apply to both the bird and the woman: cage, conditions, the oppressor, the behavior of the victim, the results.

PAIRED SOURCES ON THE IMPACT OF POSSESSIONS

We all own things we couldn't do without, maybe things we expect to be buried with. Some of our loved ones might like to bury the things first—it sometimes happens. Of course, there are the things that we'd like to get rid of, but we can't. This section pairs two writers who look back at the impact of possessions on their lives: Gary Soto and his "guacamole jacket," and Maria Varela and her "banana car."

The Jacket

Gary Soto

A writer and university professor, Gary Soto well remembers the self-consciousness of growing up. On one occasion he was all set to be cool with a fine new jacket; then his mother bought the wrong one—one that was "the color of day-old guacamole" and was "the ugly brother who tagged along wherever [he] went." Soto's best-known book is Living Up the Street.

1   My clothes have failed me. I remember the green coat that I wore in fifth and sixth grades when you either danced like a champ or pressed yourself against a greasy wall, bitter as a penny toward the happy couples.

2   When I needed a new jacket and my mother asked what kind I wanted, I described something like bikers wear: black leather and silver studs with enough belts to hold down a small town. We were in the kitchen, steam on the windows from her cooking. She listened so long while stirring dinner that I thought she understood for sure the kind I wanted. The next day when I got home from school, I discovered draped on my bedpost a jacket the color of day-old guacamole. I threw my books on the bed and approached the jacket slowly, as if it were a stranger whose hand I had to shake. I touched the vinyl sleeve, the collar, and peeked at the mustard-colored lining.

3   From the kitchen Mother yelled that my jacket was in the closet. I closed the door to her voice and pulled at the rack of clothes in the closet, hoping the jacket on the bedpost wasn't for me but my mean brother. No luck. I gave up. From my bed, I stared at the jacket. I wanted to cry because it was so ugly and so big that I knew I'd have to wear it a long time. I was a small kid, thin as a young tree, and it would be years before I'd have a new one. I stared at the jacket, like an enemy, thinking bad things before I took off my old jacket whose sleeves climbed halfway to my elbow.

4   I put the big jacket on. I zipped it up and down several times, and rolled the cuffs up so they didn't cover my hands. I put my hands in the pockets and flapped the jacket like a bird's wings. I stood in front of the mirror, full face, then profile, and then looked over my shoulder as if someone had called me. I sat on the bed, stood against the bed, and combed my hair to see what I would look like doing something natural. I looked ugly. I threw it on my brother's bed and looked at it for a long time before I slipped it on and went out to the backyard, smiling a "thank you" to my mom as I passed her in the kitchen. With my hands in my pockets I kicked a ball against the fence, and then climbed it to sit looking into the alley. I hurled orange peels at the mouth of an open garbage can and when the peels were gone I watched the white puffs of my breath thin to nothing.

5   I jumped down, hands in my pockets, and in the backyard on my knees I teased my dog, Brownie, by swooping my arms while making bird calls. He jumped at me and missed. He jumped again and again, until a tooth sunk deep, ripping an L-shaped tear on my left sleeve. I pushed Brownie away to study

the tear as I would a cut on my arm. There was no blood, only a few loose pieces of fuzz. Damn dog, I thought, and pushed him away hard when he tried to bite again. I got up from my knees and went to my bedroom to sit with my jacket on my lap, with the lights out.

6   That was the first afternoon with my new jacket. The next day I wore it to sixth grade and got a D on a math quiz. During the morning recess Frankie T., the playground terrorist, pushed me to the ground and told me to stay there until recess was over. My best friend, Steve Negrete, ate an apple while looking at me, and the girls turned away to whisper on the monkey bars. The teachers were no help: They looked my way and talked about how foolish I looked in my new jacket. I saw their heads bob with laughter, their hands half-covering their mouths.

7   Even though it was cold, I took off the jacket during lunch and played kickball in a thin shirt, my arms feeling like braille from goose bumps. But when I returned to class I slipped the jacket on and shivered until I was warm. I sat on my hands, heating them up, while my teeth chattered like a cup of crooked dice. Finally warm, I slid out of the jacket but a few minutes later put it back on when the fire bell rang. We paraded out into the yard where we, the sixth graders, walked past all the other grades to stand against the back fence. Everybody saw me. Although they didn't say out loud, "Man, that's ugly," I heard the buzz-buzz of gossip and even laughter that I knew was meant for me.

8   And so I went, in my guacamole jacket. So embarrassed, so hurt. I couldn't even do my homework. I received Cs on quizzes, and forgot the state capitals and the rivers of South America, our friendly neighbor. Even the girls who had been friendly blew away like loose flowers to follow the boys in neat jackets.

9   I wore that thing for three years until the sleeves grew short and my forearms stuck out like the necks of turtles. All during that time no love came to me—no little dark girl in a Sunday dress she wore on Monday. At lunchtime I stayed with the ugly boys who leaned against the chainlink fence and looked around with propellers of grass spinning in our mouths. We saw girls walk by alone, saw couples, hand in hand, their heads like

bookends pressing air together. We saw them and spun our propellers so fast our faces were blurs.

10   I blame that jacket for those bad years. I blame my mother for her bad taste and her cheap ways. It was a sad time for the heart. With a friend I spent my sixth-grade year in a tree in the alley waiting for something good to happen to me in that jacket, which had become the ugly brother who tagged along wherever I went. And it was about that time that I began to grow. My chest puffed up with muscle and, strangely, a few more ribs. Even my hands, those fleshy hammers, showed bravely through the cuffs, the fingers already hardening for the coming fights. But that L-shaped rip on the left sleeve got bigger; bits of stuffing coughed out from its wound after a hard day of play. I finally Scotch-taped it closed, but in rain or cold weather the tape peeled off like a scab and more stuffing fell out until that sleeve shriveled into a palsied arm. That winter the elbows began to crack and whole chunks of green began to fall off. I showed the cracks to my mother, who always seemed to be at the stove with steamed-up glasses, and she said that there were children in Mexico who would love that jacket. I told her that this was America and yelled that Debbie, my sister, didn't have a jacket like mine. I ran outside, ready to cry, and climbed the tree by the alley to think bad thoughts and watch my breath puff white and disappear.

11   But whole pieces still casually flew off my jacket when I played hard, read quietly, or took vicious spelling tests at school. When it became so spotted that my brother began to call me "camouflage," I flung it over the fence into the alley. Later, however, I swiped the jacket off the ground and went inside to drape it across my lap and mope.

12   I was called to dinner: Steam silvered my mother's glasses as she said grace; my brother and sister with their heads bowed made ugly faces at their glasses of powdered milk. I gagged too, but eagerly ate big rips of buttered tortilla that held scooped up beans. Finished, I went outside with my jacket across my arm. It was a cold sky. The faces of clouds were piled up, hurting. I climbed the fence, jumping down with a grunt. I started up the alley and soon slipped into my jacket, that green ugly brother who breathed over my shoulder that day and ever since.

Copyright © Houghton Mifflin Company. All rights reserved.

EXERCISE 7 Discussion and Critical Thinking

1. Why is the jacket more of a disappointment than it would have been if Soto's mother had given it to him as a surprise?

2. What kind of jacket did Soto request?

3. How is the jacket like a person and an evil force?

4. What are some of the failures Soto attributes to his jacket?

5. Why doesn't he lose it or throw it away?

6. What does Soto do to make this essay funny?

7. Is this mainly a description or a narration, or is it a combination with purposes integrated?

8. One might think that Soto had an unhappy, or even twisted, childhood. Do you think so? Explain.

My Banana Car

Maria Varela

To an American youngster, a first car is something to be anticipated, celebrated, and remembered. It should be the apple of one's eye, but it may be a different fruit. It could be a lemon. Even worse, as was the case for student Maria Varela, it was a "banana car." Recreated here for you, the experience is probably funnier to read about than it was to live through.

1   I remember how excited I was right after my sixteenth birthday. My dad was going to buy me a car! I imagined it would be a nice little red car with chrome rims (not hubcaps). It would have a tan interior, a sunroof, and a great stereo system that could be heard blocks away. All my friends would envy me. The good-looking boys would notice me with favor. I would be so popular. After all, the cooler the car, the cooler the car owner.

2   I could not believe what was parked in my driveway when I came home from school that Monday afternoon. It was a 1974 Chevy Monte Carlo, the kind that has the great big front end. The car was huge. It could seat forty people if it were a dinner table. To top it off, it was yellow like a banana. As a matter of fact it looked like a banana. I held my breath as I walked slowly toward the car, hoping that it belonged to someone who was visiting. At that moment my father ran out of the house with a big smile on his face. "Well, what do you think?" he said. "Nice, huh?"

3   I looked at my dad, managed to break a smile, and said weakly, "Yeah, Dad. Thanks."

4   I spent the rest of the afternoon trying to find a good quality in the car. First I looked at the outside. It had ugly hubcaps, the kind you find at Pick-a-Part for ten dollars a set. Worst of all, it had a sticker of a horse's head stuck right on the paint near the trunk. I knew that if I tried to remove it, the paint would come off and leave the outline of a horse's head in another color.

5   I opened the driver's door slowly as if something like a weasel might pop out at me from inside. The interior was light brown with dark brown stripes. It smelled like Old Spice. I got an image of the previous owner. He must have been a tall, heavy man who wore cheap cologne and liked horses. I plopped down in the driver's seat and grabbed the steering wheel with both hands. "Great!" My feet barely reached the pedals, and my nose was at the same level as the top of the steering wheel. I was a short girl, but at that moment I felt even shorter. I got a fat cushion from the house. I would have to sit on this cushion every time I drove this car. I just hoped that no one noticed I was sitting on a cushion. "Maria's so short, she can't even reach the pedals on her car." "Can you see over the dashboard, Maria?" I could already hear them tease.

6   As I drove my banana car to school the next day, I saw people staring at me. I knew what they were whispering: "How could she drive that ugly car?" and "I would rather walk," and, this one with much laughter, "I can't wait till she peels out of here."

7   To make matters worse, the car was expensive to drive and prone to breakage. It would take over seventeen dollars in gas to fill up, and that would last me only four days. One day as I was driving down the street, the muffler came off and started dragging on the ground. It made a horrible noise and sparks were flying everywhere. I knew what they were saying: "The sparkling banana car!" I was a legend. Another time I tried to open the window, but it just plopped down, never to be seen again. I could not keep anything valuable in the car for fear that it would be stolen. But, of course, I did not fear that the car would be stolen. After all, who would want it!

8   Because my banana car was so large, it was very hard to maneuver. Twice I knocked over our mailbox, which was located at the side of the driveway. I would break into a sweat whenever I was forced to parallel park. The most embarrassing situation occurred that night when my friend Monica and I went out to Tommy's. Tommy's is a popular restaurant where all the popular people from our school hang out. Monica and I decided to chance the drive-through, but as I tried to maneuver the large car up the narrow passageway, it got stuck right in the middle. There was no room to move backward or forward. I could feel my ears getting hot from embarrassment. Like the window, Monica sank down out of sight. The people behind me started

honking. I could see the people inside the restaurant looking out to see what the commotion was all about. I was ready to cry, but at that moment Danny Gurrerro, one of the cutest boys from our school, came over and asked if I needed help. "Yes, please," I blurted out. He jumped into the car and managed to maneuver it out of that tight spot. Before he left, he advised me not to take the drive-through anymore. I accepted his advice.

9   Every morning as I walked out of my house, I hoped the car would be gone, but my banana car was always there waiting for me to drive it to school. I got a part-time job at Togo's Eatery. I wanted to save money for a new car, but after two years, I still did not have enough for the down payment. One day at dinner, my father announced that since I was so responsible with my Monte Carlo, he would help me buy a new car. I jumped out of my seat and wrapped my arms around him. Then, remembering my last expectation, I backed off. "May I pick the car?" "Yes," he said. Goodbye, banana car.

EXERCISE 8   Discussion and Critical Thinking

1. What is the effect of the first paragraph?

2. While at home, how does Varela manage to conceal her dislike for the car during those three years? How does that self-control demonstrate her love and respect for her father?

3. In what way was she optimistic after she saw the car?

4. How does she characterize the previous banana car owner?

5. Is there any moment of niceness connected with the banana car?

> **EXERCISE 9 Connecting the Paired Sources**

1. To what extent do the speakers in "The Jacket" and "The Banana Car" differ in the way they regard their possession? Consider quality of the possession, peer pressure, and immediate and delayed reactions.

Reading-Related Topics for Writing About the Impact of Possessions

"The Jacket"

1. Write about the jacket from the point of view of Soto's mother.
2. Write about the jacket from the jacket's point of view.
3. Write about an embarrassing article of clothing you wore as a child, an article that you thought at the time had an influence on how others felt about you and certainly on how you felt about yourself.
4. Write about an article of clothing that you wore with pride as a child or one that you now wear with pride.

"My Banana Car"

5. Write about your first (or any other) car, one that you came to either prize or despise. Include detailed description along with discussion about the car and your life at that particular time.
6. Interview someone and write about that person's first car.
7. Write about your first bicycle or other vehicle.
8. Rewrite the essay, this time from the car's point of view.
9. Rewrite an essay, this time from the point of view of the ghost of the first owner.

Paired Sources on the Impact of Possessions

10. Write about an imaginary date between Soto and Varela, during which he wears his "guacamole jacket" and she drives her "banana car." Write from the point of view of either person or describe it from the view of an observer.

11. In "The Jacket" and "My Banana Car," the authors discuss what they dislike about their possessions. In a paragraph or short essay, discuss why they dislike and how they regard what was bought for them. Consider the questions
    - What is the importance of peer pressure—how others will regard them?
    - What is the importance of the quality of the possession?
    - Why is it important that they did not immediately reveal their disappointment?
    - With the passage of time, do these authors look back with some amusement and even pleasure? Why or why not?

ACKNOWLEDGMENTS (*continued from p. ii*)

Suzanne Britt, "Neat People vs. Sloppy People," from *Show and Tell*. Reprinted by permission of the author.

John (Fire) Lame Deer and Richard Erdoes, "Listening to the Air," from *Lame Deer Seeker of Visions* by John (Fire) Lame Deer and Richard Erdoes. Copyright © 1994 by Pocket Books. Copyright © 1972 by John Fire/Lame Deer and Richard Erdoes. Reprinted with the permission of Simon & Schuster.

Alan Thein Durning, "Seven Sustainable Wonders of the World," from *Utne Reader*, March/April 1994. To subscribe, call 800-736-UTNE or visit our website at <www.utne.com>. Reprinted with permission from Northwest Environment Watch, Seattle, WA.

Barbara Garson, "McDonald's—We Do It All for You." Reprinted with the permission of Simon & Schuster from *The Electronic Sweatshop* by Barbara Garson. Copyright © 1988 by Barbara Garson.

Ellen Goodman, "SUVs: Killer Cars." Copyright © 1999, The Washington Post Writers Group. Reprinted with permission.

Mary Ann Hogan, "Why We Carp and Harp," from the *Los Angeles Times*, March 10, 1992. Reprinted by permission of the author.

Donna Brown Hogarty, "How to Deal with a Difficult Boss." Reprinted with permission from the July 1993 *Reader's Digest* by permission of the author.

Sue Hubbell, "On the Road: A City of the Mind." © 1985 by Sue Hubbell. Reprinted by permission of Darhansoff & Verrill.

Kysha Lewin, from *Gig* by John Bowe, Marisa Bowe, and Sabin Streeter, copyright © 2000, 2001 by John Bowe, Marisa Bowe, and Sabin Streeter. Used by permission of Crown Publishers, a division of Random House, Inc.

James Lileks, "The Talkies," is reprinted with permission of Pocket Books, a Division of Simon & Schuster, Inc., from *Notes of a Nervous Man* by James Lileks. Copyright © 1991 by James Lileks.

Norman M. Lobsenz, "The Importance of Childhood Memories," from *Reader's Digest*, November 1970. Originally appeared in *Family Weekly*, October 18, 1970. Reprinted with permission of *Reader's Digest* and the author.

William Least Heat-Moon, "In the Land of 'Coke-Cola,'" from *Blue Highways* by William Least Heat-Moon. Copyright © 1982, 1999 by William Least Heat-Moon. Reprinted by permission of Little, Brown and Company, Inc.

Kesaya E. Noda, "Growing Up Asian in America," from *Making Waves* by Asian Women United of California. Published by Beacon Press. Reprinted by permission of the author.

Jennifer Oldham, "Amid Backlash, Calls for Cell Phone Etiquette," *Los Angeles Times*, July 15, 1999. Reprinted by permission of the Los Angeles Times Syndicate.

Ian Robertson, "Romantic Love, Courtship, and Marriage," from *Sociology* by Ian Robertson © 1971, 1981, 1987 by Worth Publishers. Used with permission.

Anne Roiphe, "Why Marriages Fail." Copyright © 1993 by Anne Roiphe. Reprinted by permission of International Creative Management, Inc.

Dave Shiflett, "Guzzling, Gorgeous & Grand: SUVs and Those Who Love Them," from *National Review*, June 11, 2001, v. 53, issue 11, p. 22. Copyright © 2001 by National Review, Inc., 215 Lexington Avenue, New York, NY 10016. Reprinted by permission.

Jill Smolowe, "Intermarried...With Children," from *Time*, Fall 1993, pp. 64–65. Copyright © 1993 Time Inc. Reprinted by permission.

Gary Soto, "The Jacket," from *A Summer Life*. Copyright © 1990 by University Press of New England. Reprinted with permission.

Index

abstract words, 28
"Amid Backlash, Calls for Cell Phone Etiquette" (Oldham), 42–44
analysis by division, 53–72
  examples of, 54–68
  general description of, 53–54
  topics for, 70–72
analytical definitions, 131
Anderson, A. J., 140–143
anecdote, concluding with, 5
Angelou, Maya, 19–23
annotating, 6
argumentation, 148–159
  examples of, 149–156
  general description of, 148
  topics for, 158–159
assertion, in argumentation, 151
author tags, 7

background
  in argumentation, 148, 151
  as introductory method, 5
brainstorming, 1, 41, 102
Bravo, Ellen, 133–138
Britt, Suzanne, 120–122

Cassedy, Ellen, 133–138
cause and effect, 102–117
  examples of, 103–112
  general description of, 102–103
  topics for, 115–117
childhood revisited, paired readings on, 15–23
Chopin, Kate, 173–175
circular definitions, 131
classification, 73–89
  examples of, 74–85
  general description of, 73–74
  topics for, 87–89
clustering, 1, 41, 131, 132

coherence, 2
comparison and contrast, 118–130
  examples of, 120–126
  general description of, 118–119
  topics for, 129–130
concluding paragraph, 5
concrete words, 28
conflict, in narration, 14
control, paired readings on, 74–85

definition, 131–147
  examples of, 132–143
  general description of, 131–132
  topics for, 146–147
definition of terms, as introductory method, 5
description, 28–40
  examples of, 29–36
  general description of, 28–29
  topics for, 39–40
developmental paragraph
  in comparison and contrast, 119
  defined, 3
  essay as amplification of, 5
  See also support
dialogue, in narration, 14
dictionary definitions, 131
Didion, Joan, 6–7
directive process analysis, 90
direct references, in reading-related writing, 8
documentation, 8–9
  example of, 13
  formal, 8–9
  informal, 8
dominant impression, in description, 28
Dunbar, Paul Laurence, 172
Durning, Alan Thein, 161–163

editing, 3
emphasis
  in cause and effect, 103
  in revision process, 2
Erdoes, Richard, 165–168
essays, 4–5
exemplification, 41–52
  examples of, 41–49
  general description of, 41
  topics for, 51–52
explanations
  direct and indirect, 131
  in reading-related writing, 8
expository purpose, 14
extended definitions, 131–132

first draft, 2
freedom, paired readings on, 171–178
freewriting, 1

Gallagher, Joyce, 124–126
Garson, Barbara, 91–94
gathering information, 1
general words, 28
Goodman, Ellen, 149–151
"Growing Up Asian in America" (Noda), 54–62
"Guzzling, Gorgeous & Grand: SUVs and Those Who Love Them" (Shiflett), 152–156

heritage, paired readings on, 54–68
Hogan, Mary Ann, 74–78
Hogarty, Donna Brown, 79–85
"How to Deal with a Difficult Boss" (Hogarty), 79–85
Hubbell, Sue, 29–33

imagery, in narration, 14
"Importance of Childhood Memories, The" (Lobsenz), 15–19
"In Bed" (Didion), 6–7
informative process analysis, 90, 91
informative purpose, 102, 118
"Intermarried...with Children" (Smolowe), 64–68
"In the Land of 'Coke-Cola'" (Least Heat-Moon), 34–36

introductory paragraph, 5
"Is It Sexual Harassment?" (Bravo, Cassedy), 133–138

"Jacket, The" (Soto), 178–181

Lame Deer, John (Fire), 165–168
language, 2
Least Heat-Moon, William, 34–36
Lewin, Kysha, 95–98
"Liked for Myself" (Angelou), 19–23
Lileks, James, 45–49
"Listening to the Air" (Lame Deer, Erdoes), 165–168
listing, 1, 41, 91, 102, 118
Lobsenz, Norman M., 15–19
loud talking, paired readings on, 41–49
love and marriage, paired readings on, 103–112

McDonald's, paired readings on, 91–98
"McDonald's Crew Member" (Lewin), 95–98
"McDonald's—We Do It All for You" (Garson), 91–94
meaning, in narration, 14
"Messy Are in Denial, The" (Gallagher), 124–126
mixed patterns, 160–185
Modern Language Association (MLA), 8–9
"My Banana Car" (Varela), 183–185
"My-graines" (Sheahan), 9–13

narration, 14–27
  examples of, 15–23
  general description of, 14–15
  topics for, 25–27
  using in description, 29
"Neat People vs. Sloppy People" (Britt), 120–122
Noda, Kesaya E., 54–62

objective description, 28, 40
Oldham, Jennifer, 42–44

"On the Road: A City of the Mind" (Hubbell), 29–33
order. *See* organizational patterns
orderly/disorderly people, paired readings on, 120–126
organizational patterns, 2
    for cause and effect, 103
    for definition, 131
    in description, 29
    in exemplification, 41
    in process analysis, 91
outcome, in narration, 14
outlining
    for analysis by division, 53–54
    for cause and effect, 102–103
    for classification, 73–74
    in comparison and contrast, 119
    in prewriting process, 1, 4
    for reading-related writing, 7

paragraphs, 3–4
    types of, 5
paraphrasing, 8, 9
pattern, in comparison and contrast, 119
person. *See* point of view
personalized definitions, 132
persuasive purpose, 102, 118
point-by-point pattern, 119
point of view
    in description, 29
    in narration, 14
    in process analysis, 90
points, in comparison and contrast, 118
possessions, impact of, paired readings on, 178–187
presentation, in comparison and contrast, 119
prewriting
    for cause and effect, 102–103
    in comparison and contrast, 118–119
    for definition, 131, 132
    in exemplification, 41
    general description of, 1
    in process analysis, 91
principle, in classification, 73

process analysis, 90–101
    examples of, 91–98
    general description of, 90–91
    topics for, 100–101
progress and perspective, paired readings on, 160–171
proposition, in argumentation, 148
purpose, in comparison and contrast, 118

qualification of proposition, in argumentation, 148, 151
questions
    for descriptive writing, 28–29
    as introductory method, 5, 131
quotations
    concluding with, 5
    documenting, 8, 9
    as introductory method, 5
    in reading-related writing, 8

reaction, 7
reading-related writing, 6–8
refutation, in argumentation, 148, 151
repetition, for emphasis, 2, 103
representative examples, 41
restaurants and food, paired readings on, 29–36
revising, 2–3
Robertson, Ian, 104–107
Roiphe, Anne, 108–112
"Romantic Love, Courtship, and Marriage" (Robertson), 104–107

sentence structure, 3
"Seven Sustainable Wonders of the World, The" (Durning), 161–163
sexual harassment, paired readings on, 132–143
"Sexual Harassment Is No Joke" (Anderson), 140–143
Sheahan, Vincent, 9–13
Shiflett, Dave, 152–156
shocking statement, as introductory method, 5
simple definition, 131
situation, in narration, 14

Smolowe, Jill, 64–68
Soto, Gary, 178–181
sources, documenting, 8–9
space, 2. *See also* organizational patterns
specific examples, 41
specific words, 28
"Story of an Hour, The" (Chopin), 173–175
struggle, in narration, 14
subject, 1, 3, 4
subject-by-subject pattern, 119
subjective description, 28, 40
summarizing
  for conclusions, 5
  documenting, 8
  for reading-related writing, 7–8
support
  in argumentation, 148, 151
  patterns for, 5
  revising, 3
support paragraph, 5. *See also* developmental paragraph
SUVs, paired readings on, 149–156
"SUVs: Killer Cars" (Goodman), 149–151
"Sympathy" (Dunbar), 172
synonyms, 131

"Talkies, The" (Lileks), 45–49
thesis
  in comparison and contrast, 119
  concluding with, 5
  connecting examples with, 41
  defined, 1, 4–5
  direct statement of, 5
  time, 2. *See also* organizational patterns
tone, of language, 2
topics
  for analysis by division, 70–72
  for argumentation, 158–159
  for cause and effect, 115–117
  for classification, 87–89
  for comparison and contrast, 129–130
  for definition, 146–147
  for description, 39–40
  for exemplification, 51–52
  for narration, 25–27
  for process analysis, 100–101
  for writing about freedom, 177–178
  for writing about impact of possessions, 186–187
  for writing about progress and perspective, 170–171
topic sentence
  in comparison and contrast, 119
  defined, 1, 4
  and developmental paragraph, 3
transitional terms
  for coherence, 2
  in comparison and contrast, 119
  in narration, 14
  in process analysis, 91
treatment, 1, 4
two-part response, 8

underlining, 6
units, in analysis by division, 53
unity, 2
usage, language, 2

Varela, Maria, 183–185
verb tense, in narration, 14
vivid examples, 41

"Why Marriages Fail" (Roiphe), 108–112
"Why We Carp and Harp" (Hogan), 74–78
word choice
  in classification, 73
  in description, 28
  in revision process, 2
writing process
  editing, 3
  first draft in, 2
  prewriting, 1
  for reading-related writing, 6–8
  revising, 2–3